KT-196-528

MICHAEL SCHUMACHER

Rise of a Genius

Luc Domenjoz

Preface by Jean Todt,
Ferrari Sporting Director

English version edited and translated by
David Waldron

ISBN 0-75259-228-9

© 2002, Chronosports SA
Jordils Park, Rue des Jordils 40, CH-1025 St-Sulpice, Switzerland.
Tel.: (++41) 21 694 24 44. Fax: (++41 21) 694 24 46.
E-mail: info@chronosports.com
Internet: www.chronosports.com

This is a Parragon Book

This edition published in 2002

Parragon
Queen Street House
4 Queen Street
Bath BA 1HE, UK

Copyright © Parragon

MICHAEL SCHUMACHER

Rise of a Genius

Luc Domenjoz

Preface by Jean Todt,
Ferrari Sporting Director

English version edited and translated by
David Waldron

CHRONOSPORTS
EDITEUR

Cover photo by Ollivier Hersart

Rear cover: 2000 Spanish Grand Prix (photo by Thierry Gromik)

Contents

Preface

When I took up my job at the head of the Scuderia - at the 1993 French Grand Prix - Michael Schumacher was among the outstanding hopes in Formula 1. Thus, it was natural for me to keep a very close eye on his career at the moment I was beginning the task of rebuilding Ferrari. It was a long-term undertaking that started to bear fruit during the 1994 season at the end of which we became convinced that the future lay in taking on the best driver in the world. There was only one choice: Michael Schumacher. He was then and still is today without peer.

I had met him a few years before when he drove sports prototypes for Mercedes and I was the head of the Peugeot team racing in the same championship. Let me tell you a little story: on behalf of Ferrari I met Michael in the utmost secrecy on 8th July 1995 in the Hotel de Paris in Monaco. It was in some ways our first working meeting and it lasted 12 hours at the end of which we signed a heads of agreement.

In just one day I discovered a man imbued with all the qualities that the Scuderia had a right to expect: determination, professionalism, simplicity and rigour but in addition Michael impressed me because of his exceptional maturity for his age. Thus, he became our no.1 driver in 1996 and with the passage of time I have come to appreciate another aspect of his personality. Michael is a relentless worker who gives all of himself in his job and yet he is also curious about everything. Do you know why? Because he is not only interested in himself; he cares about the needs of others which, you will agree, is rare in Formula 1! So it is not surprising that our collaboration turned into complicity. And then blossomed into friendship.

Our common approach to problems, our professionalism and our rigour have enabled us to attain our objectives. Today the Scuderia is at the very pinnacle of motor racing. Michael has won his fifth world championship title including three on the trot with Ferrari. He has also beaten Alain Prost's record number of victories. Finally, thanks to him Ferrari has racked up its fourth consecutive constructors' title.

Ferrari has now become the benchmark reference in Formula 1 and even after so many successes the team is still hungry for victory. Today, Michael happy father of two children still burns with the same passion for driving. Between races or test sessions he goes to see his kids, do some karting or spend some time with his friends.

The ambience within Ferrari is that of a dream team! We keep our feet on the ground and we cultivate humility as we know only too well the downside of things, which may lie in wait for us around the next corner. Our motivation, our passion for motor racing and for Ferrari spur us on to do everything to keep on winning so that the Tifosi everywhere in the world remain happy.

Jean Todt

Four-year-old Michael Schumacher. His first kart and collision with a lamp post!

Sutton Motorsport Images

CHAPTER 1

A mind-boggling ascension

Michael Schumacher's story began on 3rd January 1969 in the clinic of a little town in the west of Germany, Hürth-Hermühlen, where Rolf and Elisabeth Schumacher were living in a modest two-roomed flat in neighbouring Fischenich. To say that the family lacked readies would be the height of understatement!

Michael was their first child and a few months after his birth the family moved to Kerpen some 40 kms from Fischenich between Cologne and Aachen and it was here that he was bitten by the karting bug. It is a flat, mainly industrial region where fields of sugar beet share the landscape with various industries.

Michael received a very conventional upbringing steeped in the moral values drummed into him by his parents spending the odd deutschmark or two in Kerpen's cafes. At school he did not really shine and admitted to being a just a tad lazy except in 3 subjects which interested him the most: mathematics, English and Judo.

His first engine: a piece of rope!

It was outside the classroom, however, that the young German showed his talent. When he was four his father gave him a little kart with pedals like those received each year by thousands of children. At first Rolf Schumacher pulled his son's vehicle with a piece of rope and as he was a handyman he soon fitted a small engine from a scooter enabling Michael to burn up the tarmac on the pavement in front of their apartment building. Until the day he hit a street lamp - a story that has since become part of racing history! Unlike many parents who would perhaps have considered the engine-powered kart too dangerous and

forbidden their children to drive it, the Schumachers thought it was too risky to play in the streets and it would be better to do so in the right surroundings.

And so Rolf brought Michael to the Kerpen-Horrem kart track about ten kilometres from their home where he was able to drive to his heart's content as often as possible. Whatever the weather, come rain come shine, Rolf had to take his son to the track where he gradually learned to master his machine in all kinds of conditions and delighted in throwing it around in controlled slides. *"He loved spinning in the rain"*, remembers his dad.

Dad tightens the bolts and Mum doles out the chips

Today, the old track no longer exists as it was destroyed following complaints from the locals that it was too noisy. The club to which Michael belonged (and still does) moved to Kerpen-Manheim. Up to a few months ago Elizabeth Schumacher reigned over the little 'Europa Moto Drom' bar doling out chips and sausages to the region's many karting enthusiasts.

Jochen Mass, Michael's team-mate in 1990-91 (during the Mercedes-Benz era, see chapter 6) remembers his family: *"I don't really know his parents but I think they brought him up very well. The Stomachers are genuine and honest people and Michael's success owes a lot to them. Sometimes racing drivers have go-getting parents who want to do things their way. His are not like that. Michael's dad never tried to interfere with his career and he never attended races* (Michael does not like seeing his parents at a grand prix as he feels he should look after them which takes up too much time). *Rolf stayed out of all that as he knew that what was hap-*

pening to Michael and his career was beyond his control and in any case, he could do nothing more to help him."

Karting the cheapest way

Four-year-old Michael was the youngest member of the Kerpen Kart club and a year later he got his hands on a much more competitive machine. *"It was probably the cheapest kart that I'd ever seen"*, he recalls today. *"It had a 100 cc engine and my father built it up out of parts thrown away by other club members. He even had to cut the chassis as it was too long for me. But it worked and I won a few races with it."*

When Michael was seven Rolf Schumacher was offered a part-time job at the track looking after and repairing the karts. As Elizabeth was now working in the bar they were able to keep a close eye on their offspring. A year later Ralf, the younger of the two, came into the world and he too would become a motor racing enthusiast.

Club champion

In what were ideal conditions Michael soon became a karting ace and a master of controlled slides. He won his first club championship aged six and spent all his spare time racking up the laps. Even at the wheel of cobbled together karts with balder tyres, in a much worse state than those of his rivals from better-off families he won race after race.

The first problems arose when he had to have a new engine to make further progress. Its cost was 800 Deutschmarks which the family didn't have and wouldn't borrow as it was against their principles. Enter Jurgen Dilk. He was a local businessman dealing in fruit machines who had become friends with Michael. Together with some other friends in the region he began to finance Schumacher's budding career.

When the latter left school at the age of seventeen he was not particularly keen on continuing his studies. *"I really wasn't much good in any subject"*, he explains today, *"because I invested all my energy in racing and karting. What's more I hated sitting on a bench listening and learning. In 1995 when I was with Benetton and they had the Renault engine I tried to learn French but I gave up after three hours. It drove me crazy! On the other hand I loved karting when I was young and got a tremendous kick out of it and I liked football too. My hero at the time was Toni Schumacher. I was also keen on judo but of all these activities karting fascinated me the most. This being said I never dreamed of becoming a professional driver before the age of twenty."*

He finds his idol

When he was eleven his parents took him to Nivelles in Belgium, not very far from Kerpen where the Karting World Championships were being held. There the talent of a young driver, Ayrton Senna from Brazil, made a big impression on Michael and became his idol.

Thanks to some of his father's friends, especially Jurgen Dilk, who financed his new karts and equipment and brought him to the various circuits, he became German Junior Champion in 1984, an exploit he repeated the following year when he raced in the World Championship at Le Mans. Jurgen Dilk had two children and he treated Michael as if he were his own son. He is certainly the most significant person in Schumacher's success in motor racing. *"Michael already had an in-born sense of driving and mechanical sensitivity at the time"*, says Dilk. *"One day when he was racing in the German Junior Championship - he must have been around 15 or 16 - he began to have a problem on the second lap of the race. I saw him put his hand on the carburettor and keep it there throughout the race driving with only one hand. He won and then explained to me that two screws had fallen out obliging him to hold the carburettor himself. There he showed his mechanical sensitivity. I loved working with him. He had a very open mind and always listened to others' advice."*

Apprenticeship at Volkswagen

School finished Michael joined a Volkswagen and BMW dealership as an apprentice. He earned 450 Deutschmarks per month and his main job was to wash the cars and change the oil. He soon got bored with this and in addition had had to leave his family to live in Darmstadt, near the aforementioned garage. *"Living away from my parents taught me a lot"*, he recalls now. *"I had to manage my life on a very low salary. I was able to go to discos in the evening and meet girls… But I never spent more than I had."*

A free test

In 1987, after winning the European and German titles Michael, aged 18, wanted to change to single-seaters. Formula Ford beckoned but again the question of money raised its head. At the end of the season the Eufra team manager, Peter Sieber, offered him a test for 500 Deutschmarks. It was nothing more than a symbolic sum but Michael was forced to say no: he did not have the cash; neither did his father and there was no question of borrowing it. A very surprised team manager then decided to let him drive for free. His first Formula

Ford test was on the Hockenheim circuit and the way he drove that day made a big impact on Seiber.

Doing the whole season was another kettle of fish. It was out of the question to offer the young hotshoe a free drive. He had to find the money and again it was Jurgen Dilk who played the role of fairy godfather. *"I had to give the team 25000 Deutschmarks for the 10 race season"*, remembers Michael. *"It wasn't a lot but I didn't have it and Mr Dilk agreed to pay for me. For me he was father, pastor and teacher..."*

A foot in each championship

In 1988, he also raced in Formula Koenig, a low-cost series for small single-seaters fitted with wings. Finance came from Gustav Hoecker, a Lamborghini dealer, who paid for Michael's drive. Hoecker had a Formula Koënig team and he had already spotted the young Kerpen' ace's talent in the karting championships.

Even though many promising careers have been nipped in the bud when changing from karts to single-seaters such was not Michael's case. He was the 1988 Formula Koënig Champion - winning nine of the ten rounds!- finished sixth in the German Formula Ford 1600 Championship and second in the European one behind Mika Salo from Finland.

Willy Weber appears on the scene

Then came one of the pivotal moments in Michael Schumacher's career. To move up the next step in the ladder, Formula 3, he needed around 70 000 Deutschmarks. This time Mr Dilk's wallet was not deep enough. The young prodigy from Kerpen's ascension could have come to a halt there and then were it not for Willy Weber.

The latter, a rich businessman, was a keen motor sport enthusiast and had a top-level Formula 3 team entered under the WTS Motorsport banner which won the 1988 German F3 Championship with Joachim Winkelhock. A replacement was required in keeping with Weber's ambitions. *"In 1988, I went to the Salzburgring in Austria to evaluate the Formula Ford drivers,"* explains Willy today. *"One guy really made a big impact on me thanks to his style. Starting from seventh on the grid he was in the lead by the end of the first lap and I said to myself 'that's the man for my team.' I watched him for a further two races before making contact. I had him do a test and after seven or eight laps he was over a second quicker than my current driver. I signed him for 1989 and 90. He told me he had no dosh but I replied that I didn't need money, only his talent. I even paid him a monthly salary."*

There were some very hot young talents in that year's German F3 Championship including Heinz-Harald Frentzen and Karl Wendlinger. At the start of the season Michael seemed a little over-awed by the level in F3 and admitted to Christoph Schulte, one of his journalist friends, that maybe it would be better to go back to karting. *"I'm not sure I'm up to it"*, he said. This brief moment of doubt was quickly forgotten and thanks to his rapid learning curve and his reliability he was soon up among the front-runners.

A noisy and boring experience

However, the young German continued to race for pure pleasure and today he insists on the fact that at that time the thought of Formula 1 had never even entered his head. He saw his first grand prix that year in Monaco where he had come for the F3 race even though he wasn't down to drive.

The event was completely dominated by Ayrton Senna. *"I didn't race that year. Instead it was my team-mate, Frank Schmickler. The reason I went was that I knew I would probably compete the following year. I camped there with some friends. I stayed at the trackside for around fifteen minutes and it was so noisy that I had to block my ears. Then I left as it was completely boring. Driving is interesting but I get no pleasure out of standing at the side of the track watching cars pass."*

For want of a point

Finally, the German F3 Championship was won by Wendlinger (164 points) from the Frentzen-Schumacher duo (163 points each). Willy Weber brought Schumacher to Macao to measure him against the cream of the F3 drivers. The German qualified sixth for the first heat which he won but had to retire in the second due to gearbox problems. Nonetheless his performance was remarkable.

In 1990, he did another season in F3 which finished brilliantly after a disappointing start marked by accidents and incidents. In the end Michael showed he was just that bit better than his rivals and won the championship. That year he was fully occupied as in addition to F3 he had begun to drive for Mercedes-Benz in Group C. That was one of the reasons why he did not race in the Monaco F3 Grand Prix as the organisers did not want to allow a driver heavily involved in endurance to enter.

As all the pundits said competing in Group C's long endurance events was a singular choice for a youngster as it was the era when big sports car racing had become the happy hunting ground for older drivers whose F1 careers were over as well as those who were not quite good enough to make the grade in F1. This was especially true at Mercedes as among Michael's team-mates were Jochen Mass, Jean-Louis Schlesser and Mauro Baldi.

In the Mercedes-Benz Junior Team

Jochen Neerpasch, the Mercedes Competitions director, had decided to create a 'Junior Team' made up of the first three in the 1989 German F3 Championship, Heinz-Harald Frentzen, Karl Wendlinger and Michael Schumacher. All three were to back up Jochen Mass on a rotating basis while the other car was entrusted to Jean-Louis Schlesser and Mauro Baldi. The idea was to create a learning environment for the chosen three far away from the glare of the media but within a totally professional set-up the Sauber-Mercedes team.

Schumacher had several reasons for deciding to go along with this choice rather than F3000 which seemed to be a more natural step towards F1 (one used by H-H Frentzen). *"Logically speaking I should have done F3000"*, remembers Michael, *"but it was risky. Only the best two drivers in F3000 went on to F1 and you had to be with the right team. On the other hand being with Mercedes was a much safer way. I was in a position to win races. Mercedes paid me and there was a slight chance that the company would go into Formula 1."*

It was the right choice. For the three Junior Team drivers it all began on the Paul Ricard circuit beside Castellet where their first test was held. They immediately realised that they were in competition with each other and it looked like being a hotly contested day.

It was also the first time that the three young guns found themselves at the wheel of a turbocharged car weighing over a ton and putting out some 700 bhp. Finally, Michael Schumacher emerged quickest although only just from Heinz-Harald Frentzen with Wendlinger two seconds down.

The next test on the tight Jarama yielded the same results. This time they had to watch their fuel consumption which required a totally different driving style. *"We drove alternately"*, says Michael. *"Karl used too much fuel but Heinz-Harald was very quick and within the consumption limits. When I was told how much he'd used I couldn't believe my ears! So I went to the trackside to watch him lapping and I learned how to use the accelerator in a very smooth fashion to consume less fuel. This was how I drove in*

Spain in 1994 to finish second when I had only fifth gear left."

The three musketeers of the Junior Team became good friends even if Karl Wendlinger was a bit reserved. Whatever their games in the pool or on football pitches Michael always wanted to be first. " Of course I did. Heinz-Harald liked to enjoy life, have a beer, relax. He never did any muscle building. I always trained flat-out. I like eating but I watch my diet. When our trainer, the late Willy Dungl, made us run behind his car I managed to stay within 20 or 30 metres. Heinz stopped exhausted after a few minutes."

"Heinz-Harald had enormous natural talent, perhaps more than his 2 team-mates", remembers Jochen Mass, *"but Michael analysed situations, he invested more effort. Heinz did not have the same capacity for work."*

Car confiscated

Already Michael Schumacher was demonstrating amazing self-control, never indulging in excesses or doing anything stupid. He went out at night but never came home drunk. He showed exceptional maturity for someone who was just twenty-one. When asked how he managed to be so calm he replied: *"Forget my age! I've been racing since I was four, some seventeen years!"* This helps explains his error-free races as a young driver.

However, that era was not entirely without incident. One day Michael arrived very late at Le Castellet by train where his team was doing private testing. He was supposed to have come from Germany in his company car, a 2.5 litre 16 valve Mercedes-Benz. Michael had to admit that he'd been caught by the French police's radar at over 200 km/h!

The cops had confiscated his car and advised him to finish the rest of his journey (some 300 kilometres) by train. Jochen Neerpasch who never lost his cool whatever the situation, took him aside and told him that this was not the kind of behaviour expected from a Mercedes-Benz driver. Michael did not need to be told off as he'd already realised the error of his ways. It was one of the rare gaffes of his young career if one can use such a word for something so minor.

The Mercedes era wrought many changes in Michael's life. He now had a company car and his own apartment in Kerpen thus things suddenly became a lot easier. His concentration remained as steadfast as ever and when Mercedes sent him to follow a series of muscle building sessions in Austria with the late Willy Dungl, he always did more than he was asked. If Dungl advised a certain type of diet he stuck to it without the slightest deviation even though up to then he loved chocolate and his mother's Apfelstrudel. Michael did everything that would help him become a winner.

Paradise in Macao

At the end of 1990 like the previous year he went to Macao to drive for Willy Weber's F3 team with whom he'd just won the German F3 Championship. In the Portguese colony he came across Mika Häkkinen from Finland. The latter had come to Germany to race in a round of the German Championship at Hockenheim and had beaten Michael Schumacher on his home territory. It was time for revenge!

The Macao event was a magnet for the best F3 drivers from the British, French, Italian and German Championships. The race was run in 2 heats and Mika Häkkinen won the first by 2.66 secs from Michael. During the second the German managed to take the lead but the Finn was hot on his heels and obviously quicker on the straight. All he had to do was to stay in second place to win the event thanks to the addition of the times.

But Mika didn't see it that way. Nothing but outright victory would do and he launched a suicide attack on Michael Schumacher on the very last lap, hit the German's car and ended up in the guardrail. Thus, Michael won this highly reputed race and a few days later he triumphed in the Mont Fuji non-championship event pocketing the 20 000 pounds sterling promised to the driver who won both rounds. Indeed, so small was the likelihood of this happening that the money hadn't even been prepared!

A surprising gift

When he received his cheque he made a gesture that few drivers would have imitated: he gave the money to humanitarian causes. *"I wasn't that well off at the time but this money was a windfall. It came in addition to my budget and I didn't really need it. I preferred to give it to those who were much worse off than me."*

Then came 1991. Whereas Heinz-Harald Frentzen, badly advised and lacking foresight, had left the junior team and opted for F3000 (much to Peter Sauber's annoyance), Michael devoted himself to Group C racing with the Sauber-Mercedes team.

Win at all costs

That year he almost lost his self-control at Le Mans. He teamed up with Karl Wendlinger and Fritz Kreutzpointer (see photo on page 28) and decided to qualify the car, do the first stints and then take over the wheel in the closing hours of the event. He failed to realise that the race was going to last 24 hours and screwed up his chances by going too quickly. Much too quickly! During the first six hours of the race he was pushing so hard that the car's alternator broke. The team told him to slow down but to no avail. Michael wanted to win and it was one of the rare mistakes of his career due to his lack of experience in the Sarthe event. Finally, the three young drivers finished fifth.

A month later he did an F3000 race thanks to an idea of Jochen Neerpasch's who wanted his young protégé to cut his teeth in distant climes. Thus, he sent him to compete in a round of the Japanese F3000 championship on the Sugo circuit. Michael was in the same team as Johnny Herbert and Ross Cheever and finished second behind the latter. It was a case of mission accomplished and it did not go unnoticed.

In 1991, he was beginning to attain maturity. In 1990, he learned and in 1991 he went for it and was now much quicker than Jochen Mass. After Sugo he received firm proposals from two F1 teams, Footwork and Tyrrell. He did not take them up.

Four weeks after the F3000 race a set of exceptional circumstances combined to help him make his F1 debut in the Jordan team (see chapter 2). In parallel he finished his Group C season with Mercedes-Benz and came home third in the championship on the Japanese circuit of Autopolis on 27th October.

Girlfriends swap!

At the end of the 1991 season he turned up one in the paddock with Corinna Betsch, up till then Heinz-Harald Frentzen's girlfriend.

Corinna had left the latter for Michael who married her in 1995. It was the final blow for Frentzen. He had bet on F3000 with the Jordan team and money from Camel to make it into Formula 1 but in the end it was Schumacher who got this budget with Benetton (see further on), raced in F1 and nicked his girl-friend! Heinz-Harald got nothing and he still had to settle back payments to an F3 team as his sponsor of the time vanished when the bills had to be paid.

Corinna whose parents were divorced wanted security above all else. She chose Michael who now had a firm seat in F1 and lady luck seemed to smile on him.

For the youngster from Kerpen the Mercedes-Benz interlude was to prove crucial as it was there that he had learned the ropes of being a professional racing driver plus its extra-sporting activities. He was taught how to deal with the media - Mercedes had taken on a former journalist, Gustav Busing, to guide him - and with sponsors. He got to know how to set up a car and how to work with a top-class professional team. His training was complete and that is what gave the impression on his F1 debut that Michael Schumacher was the perfect driver. *"Racing with Mercedes was an unbelievable experience"*, he confirms. *"Not only did we drive cars that were very sophisticated and as powerful as F1s but also we worked with very experienced team-mates. I insist on the fact that it was with, and not against them. Jochen Mass in particular taught me a lot - and not just about driving - but about journalists, English, everything…"*

After his two seasons' training Michael was ready for the hothouse world of Formula 1. And his baptism was to be a fiery one!

Sutton Motorsport Images

On his way to winning the German Karting Championship.

Captions

His beginnings in motor sport and first kart races
Photo: Sutton Motorsport Images

Aged ten and real involvement begins
Photo: Sutton Motorsport Images

A natural born talent for driving karts
Photo: Sutton Motorsport Images

His parents Elisabeth and Rolf Schumacher
Photo: Lukas Gorys

(Top) The little bar at the circuit where Michael helped his mother serve. (Bottom) The Kerpen track
Photo: Lukas Gorys

1988: Single-seater debuts in Formula Ford 1600
Photo: Sutton Motorsport Images

1988: Parallel to Formula Ford Michael raced in Formula König
Photo: Sutton Motorsport Images

1989: Victory in Macao with Willy Weber
Photo: LAT Photographic

His relationship with brother Ralf, 6 years his junior, has always been excellent
Photo: Lukas Gorys

In 1990 Schumacher and Mass came second in the Dijon 1000 kms
Photo: Pascal Huit

First race of the 1991 Sports Prototype season at Suzuka marked by serious over-heating problems
Photo: Pascal Huit

The Mercedes Junior team warriors at Le Mans in 1991: Fritz Kreutzpointer, Karl Wendlinger and Michael Schumacher
Photo: Pascal Huit

(Top) The magic of the Le Mans pits
Photo: Dominique Leroy
(Bottom) The Le Mans race and a fifth place finish
Photo: Pascal Huit

Spa 1991: Formula 1 debuts in the Jordan
Photo: Dominique Leroy

Spa: Saturday afternoon and Michael qualifies in a sensational seventh place.
Photo: Dominique Leroy

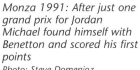

Monza 1991: After just one grand prix for Jordan Michael found himself with Benetton and scored his first points
Photo: Steve Domenjoz

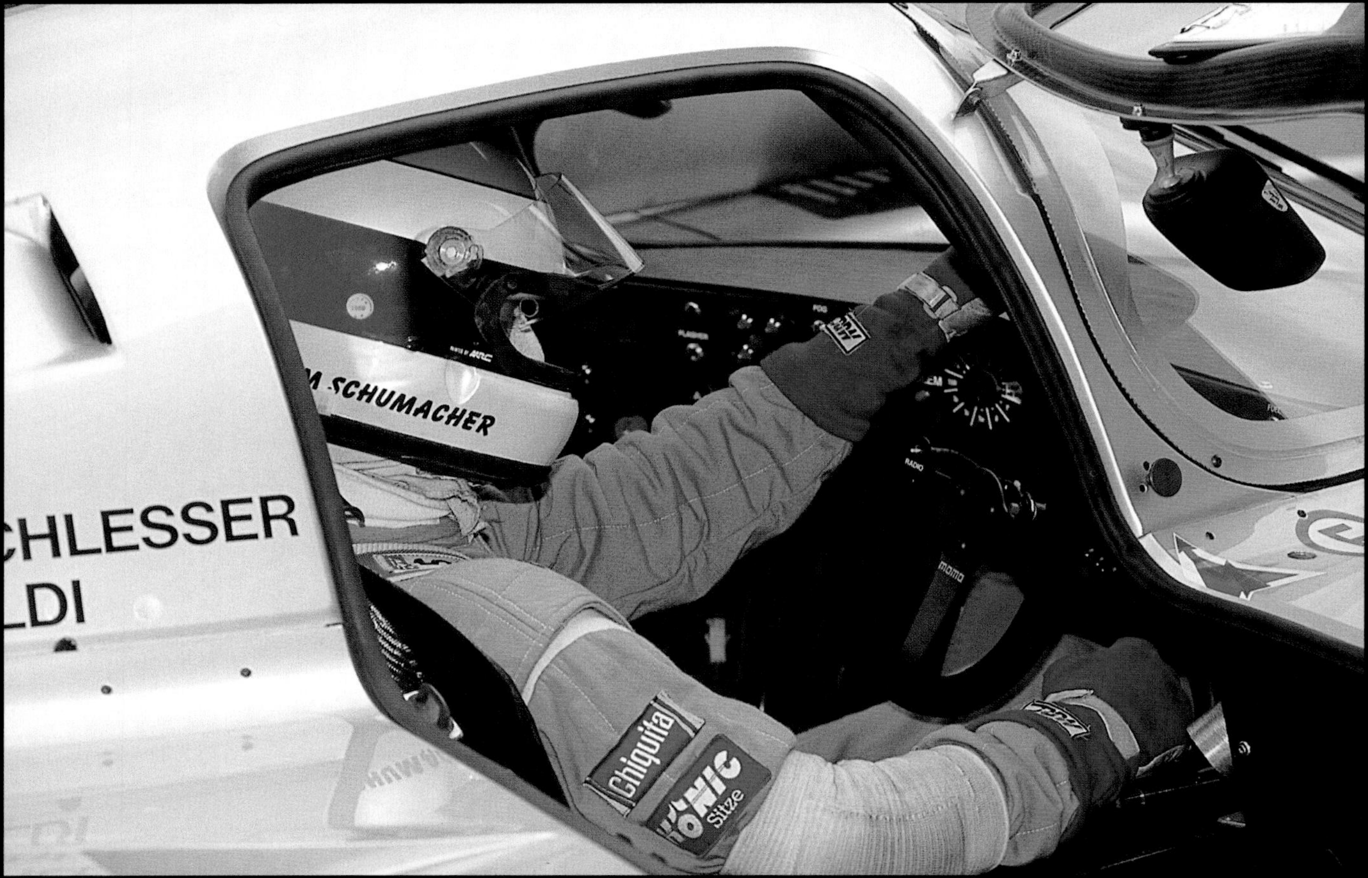
M SCHUMACHER
CHLESSER
LDI
RADIO
momo
Chiquita
Sitze

CHAPTER 2

Welcome to Formula 1!

Michael Schumacher's arrival in Formula 1 is one of the most memorable in motor racing history as much as by what happened on the track as off it! His debuts with Jordan followed by his surprise transfer to Benetton created one of the most riveting legal in contemporary F1. Now that we know that the person at the centre of the affair was destined to become a multiple world champion, the intrigue takes on its full piquancy and deserves a daily blow-by-blow account.

It all started in London on 10th December 1990 when Bertrand Gachot was on his way to the official presentation of the Jordan F1 team for which he was going to drive the following year. Along the way at Hyde Park corner he collided with a taxi. A heated argument ensued and the Belgian fearing he was in danger of being assaulted, triggered a self-defence spray in the taxi driver's face, before calling the police.

18 months for a spray

What he didn't know was that such sprays are strictly forbidden in Great Britain. Justice then took a hand in the affair and on Thursday 15th August 1991 Gachot, who pleaded not guilty, was sentenced to 18 months imprisonment with immediate effect.

Thus, Eddie Jordan found himself without a driver ten days before the Belgian Grand Prix. It was not really a problem as the Jordan 191 had proved itself to be quick right from the start of the season and drivers were banging on his door to fill the vacant seat. Eddie received numerous candidatures and in addition was negotiating with Derek Warwick, Stefan Johansson and even Keke Rosberg!

• Friday 16th August 1991

That day Willy Weber and Michael Schumacher were at the Nürburgring circuit for a round of the Group C Championship. Michael's manager then learned that Gachot was in the slammer and couldn't race in the Belgian GP: an opportunity not to be missed. Weber rang Eddie Jordan immediately whom he knew well from the F3 days - the two men even claimed to be friends! *"I've got just the guy for you for your F1 car"*, said Willy *"- Who?"*, *"- Michael Schumacher"*, *"- Who's that?"*, asked Jordan.

Feigned ignorance

Of course, like any good team manger, he was well aware of who the German was. He knew that he'd won the Macao F3 Grand Prix , the German F3 Championship and that Mercedes-Benz held him in very high esteem in Group C. So for Eddie Jordan Schumacher was a gift from the gods not to be allowed to escape at any price. Business, however, was business and it was better to feign ignorance to try and bring down the driver's market value. All the more so as Jordan wanted Michael to pay for his drive and not to pay for the privilege of running the rising star of German motor racing.

Willy Weber claims that he spent 1200 Deutschmarks that weekend on faxes and phone calls to Eddie Jordan. The Irishman wanted 150000 pounds for Michael Schumacher to drive in the Belgian race which Weber accepted to guarantee. Willy told Jochen Neerpasch, the Mercedes-Benz Competitions manager what had happened. Initially the latter was not very keen on the idea (he was already in contact with Benetton for the following season which would only come to light a few months later) but agreed. Finally, Mercedes-Benz backed the deal to such an extent that the German car manufacturer paid the money asked for by Jordan through the Sauber team. No doubt Weber was relieved that he did not have had to pay out of his own pocket.

On Sunday 18th Willy Weber and Eddie Jordan agreed that Michael would test the Jordan at Silverstone on the Tuesday before the Belgian Grand Prix. In two days time, in fact.

• Monday 19th August 1991

Michael arrived at the Jordan factory beside Silverstone to have a seat fitting; "*He seemed terribly young*", says Trevor Foster the team manager at the time

• Tuesday 20th August 1991

It was the moment of truth! Ian Phillips, Jordan's commercial director took up a trackside position on the short Silverstone circuit. "*Michael was mind-boggling that day. I've seen many many drivers on that track and we were certainly the team that used it the most. There was a dangerous left-hander and you knew how talented a driver was by his braking point. Well, after his fourth lap Michael was going through flat! It was terrifying. I asked the team to slow him down!*"

First drive

Michael Schumacher remembers his first contact with an F1 car. "*I said to myself, 'it's crazy. You're in a Formula 1 car and you're just twenty-two.' It's true that the first three laps were mind-blowing but after that everything was assimilated. Of course, an F1 was something else. It braked and accelerated quicker than anything I'd experienced up till then. But it wasn't super special. Just an extension of what I already knew.*"

• Thursday 22nd August 1991

On arrival at Spa Michael was faced with his first contractual problem with Eddie Jordan as the latter wanted him to sign a long-term deal which he refused to do. "*At that moment I said to him 'OK let's forget it' adding that I was going to bring in Stefan Johansson*", Eddie remembers. "*I didn't want to run Schumacher until the future was absolutely clear and I had an option on him for the next three years. I took a big risk entering him. I didn't want to bring him into F1, realise that he was a future star and have him snatched out from under my nose for 1992. It wouldn't have been logical.*"

However, even though threatened with being left without a drive Schumacher refused to sign the letter of intent prepared by Eddie Jordan. Jochen Neerpasch was absent that day so Michael phoned him and Neerpasch told not to sign anything but when he was told what the situation was - no signature, no drive - Neerpasch had the contract faxed to him, modified one word and sent it back to Schumacher who signed.

Two letters that changed everything

The change was the following: while Jordan's letter of intent said that Michael Schumacher agreed to sign THE contract with his team after the Belgian Grand Prix, the modification made by Neerpasch transformed the sentence into an agreement to sign A contract after the race. Thus, everything was left open as there was no allusion to any particular contract.

Jordan didn't see the trap - or maybe he didn't want to as the fact that the German had signed a piece of paper in his favour seemed guarantee enough - so Michael drove the no. 32 Seven-Up Jordan Ford in the Belgian event. The contract made provision for advertising space for Mercedes-Benz on the car and on Friday morning a man from the three-pointed star arrived to put 'TicTac' and 'Dekra' stickers on the flanks of the Jordan's bodywork.

Schumacher, however, was faced with a weekend's racing on a track he didn't know in a car with which he was barely familiar. In addition, Spa was reckoned to be the most difficult circuit of the season with fast corners like Eau Rouge which, a priori, required a lot of experience.

"*You have to go through it flat*", agrees Michael. "*At first I almost braked. Then I took it in fifth followed by sixth doing it in gradual steps and on Saturday I stared to go through flat without problems.*"

Reconnaissance on a bike!

On Thursday the German did two laps of the Spa circuit on a bike to evaluate the corners and their location. Jordan wanted his team-mate, Andrea De Cesaris to explain the track to him but the Italian arrived very late. Discussions between Jordan and the Italian dragged on and Michael never had his guided tour. Just before nightfall he rode around the 6.94 km layout again, told Trevor Foster that everything was OK, left and went to bed.

• Friday 23rd August 1991

The serious stuff began for Michael Schumacher. During the morning session he did an excellent 1 mn 55.322 secs, barely half-a-second slower than De Cesaris who had 160 grands prix under his belt! In the first afternoon qualifying run he was already almost a second quicker than the Italian in 1 mn 53.290 secs.

Underwhelmed by Alain Prost!

During this session the young debutante had to take the escape road following a slight coming-together with Alain Prost's Ferrari. He was convened by the Stewards of the Meeting and the German explained that Prost had braked far too early for the La Source hairpin. A pretty cool reaction for a newcomer!

On, several occasions the Jordan Team asked Michael if he was not driving beyond his limits and his invariable reply was that everything was under control.

• Saturday 24th August 1991

On the final day of qualifying Michael Schumacher got round in an amazing 1 mn 51.071 secs in the morning leaving De Cesaris trailing by two-and-a-half seconds. In the afternoon he was just two-tenths slower but qualified in seventh place on the grid. It was Jordan's best qualifying position of the season and it would take the Irish team three years to equal this exploit. Andrea De Cesaris was eleventh quickest and couldn't believe his eyes. *"It's impossible"*, he repeated. *"I know my best lap wasn't all that great but such a gap, no way!"*

The Italian was like a chicken without a head. Throughout the weekend he invented a whole raft of flimsy excuses to justify himself: on Friday afternoon he complained that the lower bodywork of his car was not properly fixed. On Saturday morning it was a broken gearbox which prevented him from setting up his car for the afternoon. In the Sunday morning warm up he had too much understeer and so on.

An F1? Easy to drive

"Coming here my aim was to qualify and not to get into the first ten", commented Michael Schumacher. *"I was lucky enough to start in a really good car. I never thought that an F1 could be so easy to drive!"*

That day the Jordan team realised that their debutante driver was not just another newcomer but a future world champion.

"After his first test at Silverstone we were convinced that Michael was very special", remembers Eddie Jordan. *"I've never seen another driver drive a car like him. Not even Ayrton Senna could've done what Michael did. He was just so bloody quick after the first"*

• Sunday 25th August 1991

In the race Michael's demonstration of his skills came to a sudden halt. He retired on the first lap as his clutch went 300 metres after the start. In the other Jordan De Cesaris drove the race of his life and the Italian pushed to his limits by Schumacher's performance, fought with Senna for first place!

First Grand Prix, first victory?

Andrea started from eleventh place on the grid and given the superiority of Michael and his seventh position the people from Jordan insist on the fact that Schumacher could have won his first grand prix if his car had made it to the finish. Such a victory would have been an amazing achievement as the last time this had happened in F1 was when Baghetti won the 1961 French Grand Prix in his Ferrari.

• Thursday 29th August 1991

As arranged Michael arrived at the Silverstone circuit for another test session with Jordan which went off without problems.

• Friday 30th August 1991

Ian Phillips phoned Jochen Neerpasch who confirmed that the contract was in order as agreed apart from a few minor modifications which he would have typed. The team set up a meeting with its new driver the following Monday to sign the long-term agreement discussed on the Thursday before the Belgian Grand Prix.

• Sunday 1st September 1991

Neerpasch phoned Benetton's Tom Walkinshaw to see if he would be interested in taking on Michael for the rest of the season. Walkinshaw said yes provided that there was no contract between Schumacher and the Jordan team, which Neerpasch confirmed.

• Monday 2nd September 1991

The meeting with Michael Schumacher to sign the definitive contract was scheduled for 10 a.m in the Jordan factory.

What Eddie didn't know was that during the weekend of the Belgian Grand Prix, Willy Weber had been contacted by Tom Walkinshaw. The Scot was well aware of how talented Michael was having seen him race in Group C against his own team. Tom had been with Benetton since July and had every intention of getting the German to drive for his F1 team. At Spa he told Weber that Jordan would probably not have the Ford engine for 1992 as he had negotiated an exclusive deal with the company and that the Irish squad would use the Yamaha power unit.

That put a whole new spin on things. During testing at Silverstone after the Belgian race Michael had had a long talk with Trevor Foster about the Yamaha and complained about its lack of power and excessive weight. *"I didn't want to drive with the Yamaha"*, says Schumacher. Out of loyalty he wanted to finish the season with Jordan before changing but it was impossible. His choice was now to Benetton or not to Benetton! His long-term future was at stake and his decision was quickly made.

Time flowed by and at midday there was still nobody. Eddie Jordan was furious and called everywhere to try and find Neerpasch. He finally got hold of him in the IMG offices in London (IMG is a company specialising in top level sports management). A new meeting was scheduled for 4:30 p.m the same day.

Diplomatic illness

Jochen Neerpasch arrived at the factory as scheduled with Julian Jacoby, an IMG employee. There was no sign of Michael Schumacher - according to Eddie Jordan he was already at the Benetton factory having his seat made. Neerpasch explained that Michael was not feeling well and took out a contract prepared by IMG that was completely different from the one initially agreed. As Jordan's lawyer was not present there was no question of the team accepting this new document in which were a number of obviously unacceptable clauses. Nothing corresponded to the contract prepared by Jordan in terms of space on the car, salary paid to the team and of course, the duration.

In any case according to Jordan contracts were prepared by the teams and not the drivers. And so Jochen Neerpasch and Julian Jacoby departed. Another meeting was scheduled for the morrow at 10 a.m. Neerpasch, however, contacted Benetton that evening to tell them that Michael Schumacher was free as no agreement had been reached with Jordan.

That evening Eddie Jordan also prepared a new contract which he hoped would be accepted by both parties.

• Tuesday 3rd September 1991

At 9h55, a few minutes before the meeting Jordan Grand Prix received a fax from Michael Schumacher in which he said he was very sorry but he was unable to drive for the team and that negotiations were broken off. To say that the Jordan team management was on the point of exploding would be an understatement!

Eddie Jordan then tried to find out what was going on behind his back and discovered that that very day Michael Schumacher was in discussion with Benetton. It has to be said that the latter was ready to pay the German a salary while Jordan demanded indemnities of 3.5 million dollars per year. It was also obvious that Benetton was a much better career prospect for the young German hotshoe than the Irish team.

The law intervenes

To calm things down Tom Walkinshaw got into his helicopter and went to see Eddie Jordan to whom he offered a large sum of money to bury the affair. But Eddie wasn't having any! He decided with his main collaborators that he wanted Michael Schumacher more than any cash. Thus, he appealed to the London High Court to have his rights respected on the basis of the letter signed by Michael on the Thursday before the Belgian Grand Prix. The court was to deliver its verdict on Jordan's complaint on the Thursday before the Italian Grand Prix, namely, two days later.

In the meantime Flavio Briatore met his number two driver, Roberto Moreno, at Nice airport and fired him on the spot! The motif: *"physical and moral incapacity to drive!"* The Brazilian, who had a legally binding contract, took legal action through the Milan Commercial Court to prevent anyone other than him driving the number 19 Benetton.

• Wednesday 4th September 1991

Michael Schumacher tested the Benetton on the Silverstone circuit. He covered some thirty laps without problems and that afternoon signed a contract with the team until 1995 which stipulated that Mercedes-Benz could have first call on him in 1993 if the German make decided to enter its own team in Formula 1. This was planned by the Daimler-Benz Board of Directors and Harvey Postlethwaite, a well-known British designer, had been working on the project for several months.

• Thursday 5th September 1991

On the eve of the first day's practice for the Italian Grand Prix, there was total confusion in the paddock. If Michael Schumacher was destined to become a future champion, careerwise it was obvious that Mercedes-Benz held the cards.

The hot sun that bathed the Monza park in its rays reflected the tempers in the piranha pool! Eddie Jordan had spent the morning in London trying to have his rights on Michael Schumacher respected, but the judge dismissed every one of his arguments thus no contract linked the young German to the Irish team and he was free to sign with whomsoever he wanted.

Bernie intervenes

In Milan, on the other hand, the court declared itself incompetent in the case of Moreno but condemned his team to pay him 500 000 dollars damages. Nelson Piquet, the other Benetton driver and Moreno's long standing friend, took his defence sparking off a fit of anger on the part of Flavio Briatore who threatened to fire the triple world champion and replace him with Alessandro Zanardi, a young Italian racing in F3000. It was a totally crazy state of affairs and only Bernie Ecclestone's intervention could calm things down.

He convened everybody to the Villa d'Este on the banks of Lake Como to try and find an amicable solution. He told Michael to go to bed and said that everything would be settled when he awoke.

A question of comfort

For the young German the Villa d'Este was already something special: its luxury was in striking contrast with the hole - a kind of tourist hotel like a dormitory - where the Jordan team had stayed at Spa. Thus, it wasn't surprising said the Jordan team ironically that Schumacher chose Benetton rather than Jordan.

Ian Phillips and Eddie Jordan arrived there at nine in the evening. Discussions went on late into the night between the lawyers of all the parties involved. Jordan and Phillips had a solid argument behind them, namely, to change a driver so close to a grand prix Benetton had to plead force majeur which the other teams were not willing to accept - especially Jordan. Thus, if Benetton did not want to be excluded from the championship the team had to enter Moreno. Eddie advised the Brazilian to stand up to Briatore.

Roberto, though, was persuaded to accept a 500 000 dollar leaving bonus - which Benetton was not obliged to pay - and around 2 a.m Jordan saw he had no other choice than to enter the little Brazilian for the Italian Grand Prix (he did the same in Portugal). An exhausted Eddie took a room in the Villa d'Este which he shared with Ian Phillips. They had only three hours' sleep before going to the circuit.

When Michael met Ian Phillips for the first time the next day, he showed that he was not very happy with the way in which things had evolved. *"I'm really sorry. I didn't want it to finish like that"*, said the young German to him.

Five years to forget everything

Eddie Jordan has never been one to give up easily and he undertook further legal action which dragged on for several years. In July 1996, its grounds were being judged as Jordan claimed he was the victim of severe prejudice that had considerably modified his team's history. However, before the magistrates handed down their judgement Schumacher and Jordan agreed to forget the whole affair.

The Irishman, who was no longer on speaking terms with Willy Weber, then renewed contact with him and ended up by hiring another of his drivers, Ralf Schumacher. He couldn't have Michael but at least he got Ralf!

• Friday 6th September 1991

On awakening Michael learned that all was settled. He, though, was still under a lot of pressure whether from Jochen Neerpasch, IMG or Jordan. As soon as he got into his car he forgot the outside world and concentrated on driving. He was familiar with Monza as he had raced there twice in endurance but hardly knew the Benetton.

The way he gradually brought down his lap times during the first practice session is a striking demonstration of his consistency and intelligence: 1 mn 27.725 secs, 1 mn 27.393 secs, 1 mn 27.859 secs, 1 mn 26.605 secs, 1 mn 26.042 secs, 1 mn 25.500 secs, 1 mn 25.213 secs, 1 mn 25.237 secs, 1 mn 24.656 secs, 1 mn 24.482 secs, 1 mn 24.667 secs and finally 1 mn 23.662 secs half-a-second quicker than Nelson Piquet, three-times world champion and a Benetton driver for several seasons.

In the race the German finished fifth scoring the first two points of his career. In just two grands prix he had become the little Mozart of F1.

In the following race in Portugal he scored another point before making a big impact in the Spanish Grand Prix. The Barcelona circuit was new on the calendar and a special practice session was held there on the Thursday during which Michael showed his incredible faculties of adaptation by immediately setting the fastest time of the day. In the race itself he again finished sixth.

Overall, he scored four points in his Benetton and finished the season in 13th place in the world championship. A new star was rising in the F1 firmament!

CHAPTER 3

The Carefree Years

Nelson Piquet gave up Formula 1 at the end of the 1991 season and was replaced in the Benetton team by Englishman, Martin Brundle aged 32 almost ten more than Schumacher. He had a reputation as a very quick driver who, in six F1 seasons, had never been in the right place at the right time. Now he hoped to show who was the stronger: *"Michael is very quick and I'd like to have had such self-confidence at his age. He hasn't got my experience, though. We'll work together for the good of the team but I'll do all I can to beat him. He thinks he's going to put pressure on me. That's no problem. We'll see at the end of the season."*

In fact, who was top dog was sorted out early on although here and there Martin managed to be marginally quicker than his team-mate; in particular at Silverstone where he finished third just ahead of Michael who had been faster in practice. After a very bad start to the season Brundle scored points nine times and finished sixth overall in the world championship with 38 points as against Michael's third place with 58. Compared to some of the German's future team-mates the Englishman did not do a bad job but it was not good enough and his contract was not renewed.

In the headlines again!

Michael's sudden transfer to Benetton at the end of 1991 (see previous chapter) had already spilt a lot of ink and there was more to come. On 5th February 1992, Peter Sauber sent out a press release stating that his team would come into F1 in 1993 with Karl Wendlinger and Michael Schumacher as drivers!

In the contract signed with Benetton's Tom Walkinshaw a clause stated that Mercedes-Benz had priority on the driver. However,

the German make had shelved its F1 project leaving it up to Peter Sauber to continue if he felt so inclined. The Swiss benefiting from a contract with Mercedes-Benz until the end of 1993, continued to receive a considerable sum of money from Stuttgart and had decided to make the move up to Formula 1 by himself.

At that time Jochen Neerpasch was part of the board of directors of the company 'PP Sauber AG' and he was behind the release reminding Michael Schumacher of his past commitment.

Battle for a talent

Flavio Briatore did not see things in the same light: *"Who's this Mr. Sauber"*, he roared? *"I don't know any Mr Sauber. My contract is with Mercedes-Benz, not Sauber and Michael will stay with us until the end of 1995 as agreed."* Finally, the story petered out and a friendly agreement was found. *"Michael didn't want to drive for us. Why would I have forced him"*, was how Peter Sauber summed up the situation a few months later.

The 1992 season began with the South African Grand Prix was on the revised Kyalami circuit. After qualifying sixth Michael spent half the race trying to overtake Jean Alesi's Ferrari - not easy with a Ford Cosworth. When the Frenchman retired Schumacher found himself behind Ayrton Senna where he stayed until the end. Fourth overall was not a bad result given that the Ferrari had lost a lot of oil and he had used up all his tear-offs finishing the race in a kind of fog.

Quicker than his idol

In the next race in Mexico he went one better and scored his first rostrum finish - after only eight grands prix - with a third place. *"I'd like to thank the Benetton team"*, said he with true professional calm in the post-race press conference. *"I wasn't expecting such a good result so soon."* Once again he spent a good part of the race behind Ayrton Senna: *"It was amazing to follow the world champion who was my boyhood idol and realise that I was quicker than him while trying to find a way past. I couldn't get closer than ten metres without losing all my front-end grip."* After Senna retired the way was clear for Schumacher to finish third.

Michael accuses Ayrton

In Brazil two weeks later the same trio was on the rostrum and again Michael harried Senna only now he was angry. *"At the start of the race I was quicker than him but there was no way to get past. Then he began to have problems. He was slowing and a group of cars formed up behind him. He literally prevented me from overtaking him. I said to myself that he was playing with us. I don't what his game was but it wasn't very pretty. Frankly I don't know why a three-times world champion needs to behave like that."*

What self assurance for a young driver especially as it was on the Sao Paolo circuit in front of Senna's home crowd. As Ayrton had left the circuit before the end of the race he did not hear these criticisms immediately. When he was told he replied a few months later at the French Grand Prix: *"If Michael wishes, I can show him the telemetry read-outs from Honda. He'll see what was happening with my car. But I don't give a damn about what he said. He's just a stupid kid."*

Michael Schumacher was living a dream and was always as happy as a sandboy on the rostrum swallowing large draughts of Moët&Chandon from the magnums. Barcelona saw the return of F1 to Europe and the race was run in a deluge the drivers barely managing to keep their cars on the track. Michael finished second just a few metres behind the winner, Nigel Mansell. *"I was keeping an eye on my lead over Senna and I didn't realise I was catching Mansell. And suddenly there he was just in front of me. Then he upped the pace and I let him go."* Three rostrums in three races. What a performance!

Budding popularity

This exploit grabbed the attention of all of Germany. The non-specialised press came running and at Imola the German had to give no fewer than thirty interviews during the weekend. In the race he spun and retired. Martin Brundle, who was 17 points behind the German in the championship after four races, came home fourth. He had perhaps saved his skin as rumour had it that Benetton was already thinking about replacing him.

In Monaco, on a track that he didn't yet know Michael finished fourth after a spin on the Thursday. He came second again in Montreal even though his car was not very good in the race where he was led for a time by Brundle. *"My car was oversteering unlike Martin's. Indeed, if he was a second a lap faster it was down to his car and not his driving."* Tough but true!

At the French Grand Prix relations between Schumacher and Senna took a turn for the worse. After the Brazilian's comments about Michael (see above) during practice the two drivers collided in the first corner. It was Michael's fault and he acknowledged it openly. At Silverstone he finished fourth behind Brundle.

Fisticuffs in the pits!

Before the German Grand Prix a few teams did some private testing at Hockenheim. A misunderstanding on the track with Ayrton Senna enraged Schumacher who gave the Brazilian a few brake tests! The latter returned to the pits, charged down the pit lane to Benetton and grabbed the German by the throat! The two men were immediately separated by the Benetton mechanics but there were photographers on hand to immortalise the scene. It made headlines in the German newspapers the next day. *"I suppose he wanted to give me a little massage"*, said Schumacher ironically, *"but I don't really think there's a big problem between us."*

In the race itself Michael finished third which delighted his fans who knew that the Ford was gasping for breath on Hockenheim's long straights.

Monaco: a haven

Michael moved to Monaco after the German race. not for tax reasons but to recapture the lost calm of Kerpen. *"I wasn't earning enough money for Monaco to interest me for tax reasons. When I organise a barbecue in my garden and a hundred fans jump over the fence to congratulate me, it's all a bit too much."* Monaco's advantage is that there is no room for barbecues!

In Hungary he was not in top form and in the race he retired on lap sixty-three after a collision with Brundle resulted in a spin.

First win

In Belgium he celebrated the anniversary of his arrival in F1 with his first victory. After only twelve months he had got the measure of his car. *"I felt it coming,"* were his first words on leaving the rostrum. *"This morning in the motorhome I suddenly felt intuiti-*

vely that I could win here. The car was much better in the race than in qualifying and I'd like to thank the team yet again."

It wasn't an easy race. After ten laps he was fourth and on lap thirty he made a mistake and went off briefly. He rejoined behind Brundle. *"That off was lucky. When following Martin I noticed that his rain tyres were blistering and I though it was time to fit slicks. I was the first to come in and it was the right choice."* As the race ended Mansell's Williams was reeling in the German's Benetton that was now in the lead. The Brit's car ran into exhaust problems and Michael was on his own. *"At Hockenheim when I finished third, on the rostrum I felt tears in the corners of my eyes. This time I wept openly. I am just so happy."*

Happy is probably the most appropriate adjective for this period in Michael's life as he went from success to success. At the end of the season he finished on the rostrum at Monza and in Adelaide. In just a year the 'little Mozart' of Formula 1 had proved that he was made of the same right stuff as all the other great champions. He seemed overwhelmingly talented and with his speed, race sense and technical ability a brilliant future beckoned. And so it proved.

At the start of the 1993 season Benetton moved from its Witney factory to its new premises at Enstone, an ultra- modern building where the team could plan for its ultimate objective, the world championship title.

Experience called on

In the driver line up Martin Brundle had been replaced by Ricardo Patrese, Nigel Mansell's partner the previous year. The Italian was a real veteran whose F1 career had begun in 1977. The Benetton team management judged that he would provide their young prodigy with the experience he lacked. They were wrong all down the line as in 1993 Patrese was literally made a laughing stock of by his team-mate. At Silverstone for example, Michael got into Ricardo's car and without adjusting the set-up was two seconds quicker than the Italian. The latter was totally demoralised and retired at the end of the season.

Michael was now twenty-four and looked to have a rosy future ahead for him but the only cloud on the horizon was the Ford Cosworth engine, which powered the Benettons and did not seem to have the grunt to enable him to do battle with the best. *"I've been in Formula 1 for a year and a half. I've learned a lot but I've still got a lot to learn. It's a fact that the majority of drivers who've won the championship have taken about five years to do so."*

Corinna was now living with him in his two-roomed flat in Monaco. In June the couple moved into a bigger apartment still in the Fontvieille quarter. During the 1992 season Michael complained about the fact that he was battling with Senna and Mansell who were both earning millions while he had to be content with 250 000 dollars per year. In 1993, his salary was increased and he was now the Benetton team leader. *"I've got less time for myself and there's more pressure,"* he admitted. *"I can cope but sometimes I'm a bit sharp with people which is something I detest. I have to do it otherwise I'd have no time for myself at all. I think I'm still the same as before but I have to adopt to new circumstances. Formula 1 is thought to be a little PR and a lot of driving but it's the opposite; a lot of time for public relations, sponsors and the press and a little bit of driving!"*

The happiest man in Formula 1

In 1993, he finished more often than not on the rostrum and still showed that natural joie de vivre when spraying the champagne. He was described as the happiest man in Formula 1 by several magazines and he obviously revelled in his existence. *"My ambitions are not that great,"* he explained at the dawn of the season. *"I'm a bit cautious on this subject. I suppose that my ambition is to be successful and happy in F1. For the longer term, I don't know. Maybe I'll go back to karting. Who knows? When I think about life at fifty I see myself somewhere calm and certainly not in F1. Or completely in the background."*

Kyalami in South Africa again hosted the opening round of the 1993 championship. It was here that Michael revealed himself as the main threat to Ayrton Senna and Alain Prost, the two stars of the moment. In theory the Benetton team had the best Ford engines by contract but McLaren and Senna dropped by Honda did everything in their power to show that they were worthy of as much attention as Benetton. The pressure was tough and hard to bear at times.

For Benetton it was not an easy year. The team brought out a completely new car for the third grand prix of the season on the Donington circuit. For the first time the B193 had electronic suspension and driver aids which were already on the McLarens and Williams. Precious time had been taken up getting these gizmos right.

Knee problems

Michael himself was not in as good shape physically as in 1992. A chronic knee problem prevented him from training as much as he wanted and in fact, he had to have an operation the following winter to solve the problem. On the track he again crossed swords with Ayrton Senna especially at Kyalami where both cars touched: then at Spa where he accused the Brazilian of having deliberately pushed him off the circuit. At the end of August of that year Senna and Frank Williams were involved in discussions about Senna driving for Williams in 1994. Flavio Briatore had also offered Ayrton a seat in his team which the latter said he would think about but only used it to up the ante in his negotiations with Frank.

Michael Schumacher gave full vent to his opinion about the possible arrival of the Brazilian in his team. *"I think that Ayrton would destroy the ambience that exists in Benetton. He's done the dirty on me on several occasions which I don't accept. Maybe he believes that I'm the only one who can beat him and that's why he's so tough with me."*

In the end the 1993 season did not add much to Michael Schumacher's talent but deepened his experience. He won only one race, the Portguese Grand Prix and was in the points nine times (all rostrum finishes) finishing fourth in the world championship with 52 points.

CHAPTER 4

1994: A marked man

After a couple of learning years (1992-93) Michael was now a probable world championship contender and in addition 1994 was a year of renewal for Benetton. The brand-new B194 chassis was the first to have been built in the new Enstone facility inaugurated by Benetton the previous year.

Enginewise Ford and Cosworth had made an enormous effort by building the V8 Zetec-R said to develop as much power as a V10 but more torque. Commercially Benetton had left its traditional sponsor Camel, replacing it with the Japanese brand Mild Seven. Thus, the familiar green and gold livery metamorphosed into shades of blue.

First fruits

Michael's standard of living was on the rise. Having moved into a bigger apartment still in the Fontvieille district of Monaco he bought himself a Mercedes-Benz 500SL, a Ferrari F40 to which he added a Bugatti EB110 SS a few months later. During the winter he had had his knee operated on to cure the problems that arose in 1993 and he was now totally recovered.

Indeed, he had been approached by Ron Dennis during the winter as the British team manager wanted him to join McLaren-Mercedes for the coming season. The financial conditions were very attractive but Michael, helped by a salary increase, preferred to stay with Benetton the team with which he had grown up.

"My aim this year is to establish Benetton as the number 2 team," was how he analysed the situation during the winter. *"My driving motivation is to beat Senna and Williams who, in my opinion, are the favourites for the championship. With a bit of luck, we can put them under pressure and win the odd race, but for the championship itself, we're maybe not yet up to their level."*

The regulations too had changed a lot since 1993 as all driver electronic aids were now banned, a situation with which Michael was very happy.

A black year

The 1994 season will forever remain in people's memory as a tragic one due to the deaths of Roland Ratzenberger and Ayrton Senna. It was also marked by Michael Schumacher's total domination which turned to farce during a controversy-filled summer.

Michael's role after Senna's death wasn't as easy as it seemed. After the Brazilian's fatal accident it was difficult to see who could challenge a driver having already won the first three grands prix of the season with such ease that he seemed to be in a class of his own. Thus, his title looked to be a mere formality. The begrudgers of course said that his would be a flawed crown in the absence of Senna.

Thanks to the exceptional brio which he showed in Monaco, first of all and then in Spain where he finished second in spite of his car being stuck in fifth gear for most of the race he silenced his critics and proved that he was a worthy successor to Alain Prost as the year wore on.

Twelve against sixteen

In 1994, the German had twelve occasions on which to score points as against sixteen for Damon Hill because of the numerous polemics that besmirched the season (see below). This in itself more than justifies Michael Schumacher's F1 world title.

With the exception of Silverstone he proved that he was the best driver on the track in 1994. Only the mistakes of the Benetton team and the severity of the FIA's judgements allowed Hill to catch up with him at the end of the year, a situation that seemed unfair given the talent of the German driver. The FIA, anxious to keep interest in the title battle alive until the very end, manipulated the situation perfectly.

Michael and Damon arrived in Australia almost equal and fought a mind-blowing duel in the streets of Adelaide until a collision eliminated them both.

A few metres make the difference

Finally, after sixteen grands prix, the result was decided in just a few metres. And for once Lady Luck smiled on Michael. Not before time as up till then it had all gone wrong for him.

He had had an awesome start to the season. In Brazil, the first round, his duel with Senna had turned in his favour during the refuelling stops. 1994 marked the return of refuelling to Formula 1 and the Benetton team had rehearsed the manoeuvre hundreds of time throughout the winter which was obviously not the case with Williams.

At the start of the race Michael shadowed Senna waiting for the first stops to take over the lead and keep it. *"Once I was in front I was able to control the gap with Ayrton fairly easily,"* said the German. *"When necessary I could push a little harder."* First grand prix, first win for Schumacher. *"It's great to start like this. All the credit goes to the team and to Ford who've both worked like crazy during the winter."*

He also won the second grand prix of the year was on the Aïda circuit in Japan after Senna on pole was taken out in the first corner by Nicola Larini's Ferrari.

The season looked like being a nail-biting duel between the German and the Brazilian and then came the San Marino Grand Prix at Imola where Ayrton Senna met his death. Michael's team did not tell him what had happened. He won the race but it was a victory he would willingly have done without. *"I didn't know what had happened. Among the drivers Eric Comas was the only one who knew the truth as he had stopped beside the remains of Senna's Williams. It was obviously a heavy impact but having already seen so many in F1 that did not have serious consequences, I had no idea it was so bad."*

State of shock

Finally, it was Willy Weber his manger who told Michael that Ayrton was dead. *"He was terribly shocked by the news and began to cry like a baby,"* said Weber.

Michael blamed himself for Senna's death as he had pushed him to his very limits, and had to be consoled by the Benetton team. He admitted that he spent several sleepless nights over the next few days.

The deaths of two of his rivals was as big a shock for Michael as it was for the other drivers. It reminded all those who had forgotten just how dangerous F1 could be. Initially, Michael did not know whether or not to pursue his career or stop. He spent a few days holiday on board Flavio Briatore's yatch before having a private test session at Silverstone which showed him that he was as quick as ever (see chapter 11).

In Monaco he scored his fourth consecutive win of the season and it was increasingly clear that no one could match his pace. This event was the scene of Karl Wendlinger's terrible accident on Thursday morning. The Austrian in a coma was transported to a hospital in Nice where he remained for many days. Something had to be done about safety in Formula 1 as the situation was extremely grave.

Wrong decision

The drivers' decided to revive the GPDA, their old association and Michael Schumacher played a leading role in it. Nonetheless he refused to go to Sao Paolo for the funeral of his rival. *"At the time I didn't go because I was afraid for my safety but above all what was the point of going to a church to show what I felt. Ayrton was my boyhood idol and my feelings about the rest of my career were somewhat confused. But I now regret I didn't go. I think I took a wrong decision ."*

In fifth only

Two weeks after Monaco Michael scored a brilliant second place in the Spanish Grand Prix as his car was blocked in fifth gear for most of the race and he had to refuel twice. Towards the end he lapped in 1 mn 26 secs, a time identical to the other drivers on the track. That day was a better demonstration of his talent than if he had scored another victory.

In Canada he notched up his fifth win of the season leading from start to finish and he did the same at Magny-Cours. By mid-season he led the championship by 37 points from second-placed Damon Hill.

Then things started to go wrong. In Formula 1 it's not always a good thing to dominate outrageously. With Michael Schumacher having won six out of seven grands prix public interest in a championship whose outcome seemed a foregone conclusion, waned. Viewers zapped to other programmes and the sponsors lost part of their audience thus reducing their budgets and F1 began to feel the heat.

This explains why Michael Schumacher became a marked man. His slightest error was to be harshly punished and unfortunately his team made some monumental ones. It was a stormy summer for Benetton.

• San Marino Grand Prix: 1st May 1994

Ayrton Senna's dramatic death did not prevent the International Automobile Federation (FIA) from pursuing its work. It suspected that several teams were cheating in the area of traction control which had been banned. Thus the FIA asked teams to send it copies of their engine management programmes immediately as it was in these that an undetectable traction control system could be stored. McLaren did as told but Benetton dragged its feet and sent in the documents three weeks late which could have allowed the team time to falsify them.

It was very difficult to check these documents as for a computer expert to pierce the secrets of a programme written by someone else is an almost insurmountable task. As enough evidence could not be gathered to prove that Benetton was cheating the team came out of the affair in the clear. The FIA, though, was still sceptical and did not hesitate to say so thereby calling into question Michael Schumacher's early-season superiority which, said the doubting Thomases, could only come from an illegal system. The FIA continued to keep a close eye on Flavio Briatore's team.

• French Grand Prix: 3rd July 1994

At Magny-Cours Michael made such a perfect start that he substantiated the theory he had traction control. It was even possible that the German was not aware what his team was doing behind his back.

• British Grand Prix: 10th July 1994

Michael Schumacher passed Damon Hill during the formation lap and was given a five second stop 'n' go penalty which he did not respect. He was then shown the black flag for three laps but refused to stop.

What he did during the formation lap was not very serious as drivers have always passed each other during this lap without being penalised. The German explained that he overtook Hill when the latter braked so as not to flat-spot his tyres. His explanation did not hold water as the TV showed that the overtaking move was done under acceleration. "*Of course I passed Damon and it was against the regs but I was totally unaware of this rule. Usually , nobody had a problem.*"

The problem, in fact, was that the Benetton team at the moment the 5 second penalty was inflicted (at 14h27 to be exact) tried to negotiate its suspension. Flavio Briatore and Tom Walkinshaw went to argue with Race Control. The driver was warned of the sanction but it seems that the on-board radio was not very clear. Michael thought that the time would be deducted at the finish as used to be the case.

Black flag

On lap 21 Michael was shown the black flag three times which he ignored. He later explained that he did not see it whereas in fact Briatore and Walkinshaw, who were trying to cancel it, told him to stay out. As their plea fell on deaf ears the German was told to come in on lap 27 which he did and finished the race in second place.

Race Control thought that Michael was being economical with the truth and fined him 25 000 dollars for not knowing the regs.

Following these events the FIA opened an inquiry. Depriving Michael of his 6 points and suspending him were evoked as Nigel Mansell had been given the same punishment in similar conditions in 1989.

• Tuesday 26th July 1994

Following the British Grand Prix the World Council of Motorsport held an extraordinary meeting in Paris and decided that Michael Schumacher had committed a very serious fault by ignoring the black flag. It did not believe his explanation saying that he had seen the number 5 (his own) but not the flag and thought it meant 5 seconds. "*It is a very serious matter when a driver who does not stop for the black flag,*" hammered home Max Mosley. "*It's like a football player who's given a red card and refuses to leave the pitch.*"

Schumacher was suspended for 2 grands prix, lost his Silverstone points and the Benetton team was fined 500 000 dollars. "*I think it's a lot of hot air for nothing and I don't feel it's right to interfere in the championship like this,*" were Michael's comments.

To ensure that Michael was present for the German Grand Prix thus saving the race as all seats had been sold to his fans Benetton appealed the decision risking a heavier penalty.

• German Grand Prix: 31st July 1994

Michael was forced out on lap 21 when his engine lost all power but for Benetton the worst was still to come.

During refuelling Jos Verstappen's car caught fire. It was quickly extinguished but could have had very serious consequences as the driver and four mechanics were badly burned. In the inquiry that followed the French company, Intertechnique, which manufactured the refuelling equipment supplied to the teams discovered that one of the valves in the pipe had been removed by the team which thought it would thereby gain a second during refuelling. The removal of this valve was the probable cause of the fire thus the FIA threatened to disqualify the team from the championship. It was the pits for Benetton.

• Hungarian Grand Prix: 14th August 1994

The paddock's sole topic of conversation topic was the Benetton affair as once again Flavio Briatore's team was playing with fire both literally and metaphorically. It argued that it had asked Charlie Whiting, the FIA technical delegate, to be allowed to modify the refuelling system. *"I said that so far as I was concerned there was no problem but they had to ask Intertechnique's permission,"* explained Whiting in Budapest. Without doing so Benetton used its modified system during the race and Verstappen's car caught fire.

On Thursday in Budapest Intertechnique's representatives said that the only way to modify their system was to send them a letter asking permission. No request had been received from Benetton and furthermore they would never have authorised the removal of a safety filter. Thus there was deliberate cheating.

Benetton tried to defend itself and on Saturday handed out a press release saying that the Hockenheim fire had been caused by a fault in the equipment supplied by Intertechnique. In fact in the Budapest paddock technicians from the company had been seen changing the valves on all the teams' rigs. Whether or not the fire came from equipment failure did not efface the attempt to cheat.

Benetton excluded?

Following this affair the FIA executive saw red and threatened to simply exclude Benetton from the 1994 Championship for having endangered the German Grand Prix. The case was to be judged before Monza by the World Council.

Benetton had taken an enormous risk to gain a second during refuelling and in Budapest Schumacher refused to comment. *"The team hasn't cheated as we've already proved with the traction control affair,"* was all he would say in the paddock.

On pole in the hot seat

Given the problems that were destabilising the team Michael set a remarkable pole position time which showed his ability to cope with stress. Sunday confirmed this as he won the Hungarian Grand Prix. It was a pleasure to see his delight after the race. Hardly had he got out of his car than he punched the air as a sign of victory.

His success made him forget his woes (temporarily at least). He jumped for joy on the rostrum and in his excitement went to the toilet completely forgetting the post-race press conference where over a hundred journalists were waiting to hear his impressions. Hauled back by the organisers he finally arrived: *"It's fantastic to win here especially given the pressure I've been under this weekend. But I'd really loved to have been in this spot two weeks ago in Hockenheim. Of course there are a lot of German fans here but it's not like being at home."*

He had a trouble-free race. He hit the front from the green light, refuelled without problems and won. Damon Hill finished second more than 20 seconds behind the Benetton a gap that Schumacher could have widened if necessary.

• Belgian Grand Prix: 28th August 1994

A few days before the Belgian Grand Prix, the English Sunday paper 'The Observer' said that Michael Schumacher was ready to quit the Benetton team if it was true that the refuelling equipment had been tampered with. *"For me honesty is the most important quality,"* he affirmed stating that he couldn't bear the idea of benefiting from cheating.

The Tuesday before the Spa event Benetton announced that it had signed a contract with Renault for 1995. This good news was quickly pushed aside by the Belgian Grand Prix affair.

The regulation changes brought in after the Imola accidents included the introduction of a wooden plank on the bottom of the cars in order to banish any form of ground effect. This plank had a 10 mm thickness with a tolerance of 1 mm.

On the Spa circuit Michael came home an easy winner. This increased his points total to 86 as against 51 for Damon Hill. When Michael left the rostrum he was a happy man. The Belgian circuit where he had scored his first grand prix win in 1992 after his debut there a year earlier, was once again the theatre of another success. *"I love this track as it's the nearest to my home and all my fan club is here whom I would like to thank for their support,"* he commented.

After opening up a big gap over his pursuers in the early part of the race he then slowed down. And spun through 360 degrees over a kerb! *"I was a bit surprised"*, said the German. *"As we had hardly any practice in the dry we adopted rule of thumb settings and they were far from ideal. At the start the track had no grip but it improved as the race wore on. When my car spun I let it go through 360 degrees. It's the type of thing you get used to. On coming out of it I was able to choose the direction to go in and there were no problems."* At that moment Schumacher did not know that his manoeuvre was to cost him victory!

Four hours after the end of the race the news broke: the German was disqualified for excessive wear of the flat bottom. Most of the front part, around 25% of its length, measured no more than 7.4 mm, 1.6 mm under the legal tolerance.

Hill profits from disqualification

The Benetton engineers justified the deficiency in vain by their driver's spin in the race - which was responsible for tearing off the wood on the kerb - but disqualification was pronounced and Hill declared winner reducing the gap between the two men from 35 to 21 points.

"There are times in your life when you wonder what you've done to God to merit such a fate," said Schumacher the next day. *"First of all I didn't want to believe it. I'd really driven my heart out and I was completely devastated to learn that I'd been stripped of one of the best wins of my career. As I wasn't on the spot I was at a loss to understand what had happened but one thing I'm certain of is that neither myself nor my team cheated to try and gain any advantage. Why would we? Even Damon Hill admitted our superiority by congratulating us at the end of the race."*

Schumacher's main fault seems to have been that he finished first as it is possible, indeed probable, that several other cars had their flat bottom damaged by going over the numerous kerbs on the circuit. *"All I know is that it was very difficult for all the dri-*

vers to find the right ground clearance settings as we hadn't done enough practice in the dry."

Michael felt very down in the mouth as he also had to face the FIA Appeal Court on the Tuesday following the race. *"For sure, I'll try and stay relaxed. One day Lady Luck will smile on me."*

• Tuesday 30th August 1994

The judgement handed down in the first instance against the German driver was confirmed by the FIA's Court of Appeal thus Michael was banned from taking part in the Italian and Portuese Grands Prix on 11th and 25th September.

He was expecting this decision even if at Spa he said that he hoped the judges would show a little clemency but admitted that his team had made a blunder.

This meant that the way was open for Damon Hill to claw back a large chunk of his 21 point deficit. His only rivals at Monza and Estoril were the Ferraris and victory in both races would bring him to within one point of the German.

The accusations of cheating during refuelling were to be judged on the following Wednesday, just before the Italian Grand Prix. Michael admitted to a German newspaper 'Welt Am Sontag' that he would leave Benetton if these proved true. If this were so then both driver and team could quite simply be excluded from the championship. Benetton was on the razor's edge.

• Wednesday 7th September 1994

"The FIA World Council judged that the Benetton team had not tried to cheat by removing a filter from the refuelling rig of Dutchman Jos Verstappen's car during the German Grand Prix on 31st July". This put an end to the Sword of Damocles hanging over the team. It was, however, established that it had removed the filter without authorisation to try and gain a second during refuelling but the FIA did admit that things were not as clear as they seemed.

First of all the people from the French company Intertechnique, which made the refuelling rigs for all the teams, did not come to the Benetton factory until three days after the Hockenheim fire thus leaving the team members enough time to put back the filter in question. According to the FIA the fact that this had not happened was proof of the good faith of the English outfit.

In addition, Flavio Briatore, the boss kept repeating that all the teams except four had removed the filter. The FIA had been surprised to learn on Tuesday evening that

Intertechnique had authorised the French outfit Larrousse to remove the part in question in May!

Finally, Briatore said the Benetton management was not aware of the removal of the filter a decision taken by one of the team engineers which he judged not worthy of mention. Indeed, one of the FIA inspectors had given his agreement to this modification but it turned out that he did not have the competence to take such a decision.

The Italian then added that his team had filtered the fuel twice before pouring it into the refuelling rig thus the fire could only have been caused by a defect in the Intertechnique equipment.

Given the complexity of the affair the World Council preferred to absolve the team: it was a wise decision and the only one possible.

Ten points less confirmed

The World Council, however, confirmed Schumacher's disqualification pronounced on the evening of the Belgian Grand Prix. He now had only 21 points in hand over Damon Hill and was forbidden to take part in the Italian and Portguese Grands Prix. Thus, the British driver was the only real obstacle between Michael and his first world champion title.

Damon did what was asked of him and won both the above-mentioned events so with three races to go, the European, Japanese and Australian Grands Prix Hill was back to within one point of the German. It was going to be a thrilling end to the season.

During his enforced absence from the track Michael Schumacher went training in the Swiss Alps to be in the best possible form for the end-of-season battle.

Winning comeback

He dominated the European Grand Prix on the Jerez circuit winning from Damon Hill. *"It's exactly what I wanted,"* he said happily. *"To take up where I left off at Spa, namely, winning by a large margin. The whole team has been remotivated."*

At Suzuka, the second-last round of the championship was hit by rain and to everybody's surprise Damon Hill won in conditions that were ideal for Schumacher beating the German by three seconds. Yet again the latter was quickest in practice but he lost the race due to an error on the part of his team as he was on a two-stop strategy which was spoilt when the event was run in two heats following an accident involving a Japanese marshal and the final result decided by adding the two times.

And so the rivals turned up in Australia separated by a single point: 92 for Schumacher and 91 for Damon Hill.

An historic collision

The early part of the race saw a sensational duel between the two men which ended prematurely on lap 36. Michael Schumacher, who then had a tiny lead over Hill, went off and kissed the concrete wall. He got back onto the track leaving a gap on the inside in the next corner which Hill tried to go through. It was a very tight right-hander and Michael closed the door leading to a collision between the two cars and their elimination. But the German had done enough to win his first world championship.

In fact, had Damon waited another few metres he could have gone into the lead and won without problems as Michael Schumacher's car had been damaged in the first impact. The Brit didn't know this and went for broke losing everything in the process.

Alain Prost defends the German

Certain pundits said that Michael had deliberately provoked the accident knowing that his race was run. Alain Prost's expert view, on the other hand, contradicted this as he said that Schumacher had only done his job as a driver by attempting to hold of Damon Hill: *"Michael showed that he was a real racer. He turned in and closed the door instinctively. It was all he could do at that moment. It was self-defence and not an attacking move."*

With his world title in his pocket Michael did not forget to render a last homage to Ayrton Senna: *"Winning this championship is like a dream for me,"* were his first words that day in Adelaide. *"I feel the emotions but I don't know how to express them. It was clear to me that I would not win it this year and that the title would fall to Ayrton Senna. But he's not here any longer so I would like to give him this world title which he should have won. He had the best car and he was the best driver. I've often thought of him this season even if I don't often show my feelings."*

For Michael Schumacher it was time for a few days holiday. He hoped that the 1995 season would be free of controversy as the 1994 one had been mentally very exhausting.

Captions

1992: Brazilian Grand Prix. Michael Schumacher's second rostrum finish!
Photo: Steve Domenjoz

1992: In the rain at Spa on his way to his first win
Photo: Steve Domenjoz

His joy on the rostrum after winning his first grand prix
Photo: Steve Domenjoz

1992: The birth of one of the future stars of motor sport
Photo: Steve Domenjoz

1993: His new team-mate, the very experienced Ricardo Patrese, whom he quickly demolished
Photo: Dominique Leroy

The 1993 South African Grand Prix: Michael battling it out with Ayrton Senna and Alain Prost
Photos. Dominique Leroy

(Top) On the way to second place in front of his home crowd at Hockenheim
Photo: Steve Domenjoz
(Bottom) Pushing hard in the Parabolica at Monza
Photo: Dominique Leroy

1993: Last race of the season in Adelaide
Photo: Dominique Leroy

1994:The Brazilian Grand Prix with Michael Schumacher getting the new season off to a flying start
Photo: Dominique Leroy

(Top) Victory at Spa before being disqualified.
Photo: Dominique Leroy
(Bottom) Monaco victory
Photo: Steve Domenjoz

1994 Hungarian Grand Prix: Michael treads his way through controversy
Photo: Steve Domenjoz

(Left) Michael salutes the Hockenheim crowd during the drivers' parade.
(Right) Victory joy with Flavio Briatore
Photos: Steve Domenjoz

Jerez: signs of reconciliation between the two 1994 rivals
Photo: Steve Domenjoz

1995: Another Monaco Grand Prix win
Photos: Steve Domenjoz (top) and Dominique Leroy (bottom)

1995: Victory on the Hockenheim circuit. Frenzy on the rostrum and in the crowd
Photos: Steve Domenjoz

The Nürburgring 1995: Punching the air with the 1995 title almost assured
Photo: Steve Domenjoz

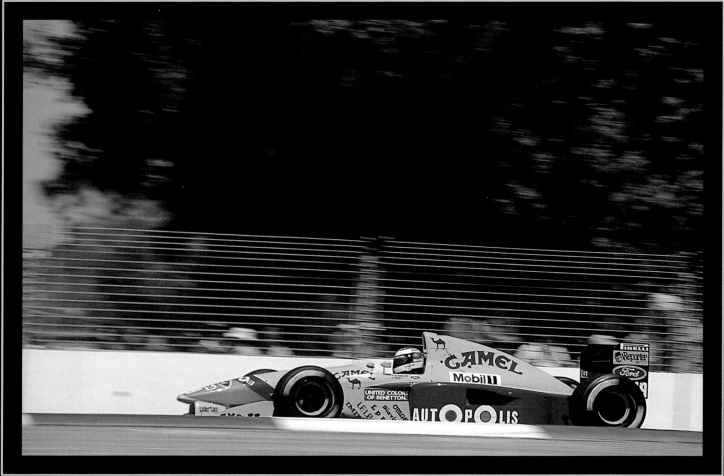

CHAPTER 5

Nine victories confirm his talent

In 1995, Michael Schumacher wanted to put behind him the controversy that had surrounded his first title. His Benetton was now Renault-powered enabling him to do battle with the Williams on an equal footing.

On paper anyway his main rival was Damon Hill in his Williams-Renault but it was difficult to see how the British driver could beat the German in 1995 if he had not managed to do so the year before when he had a much better engine, and the sporting powers had done their utmost to put a spanner in Michael Schumacher's works (metaphorically speaking, of course)!

However, it was not all plain sailing for the young German as the Benetton 195 proved to be a capricious machine compared to the Williams. It needed a perfectly smooth track to give its best and he complained of chronic understeer in qualifying. Generally the problems affecting the car during practice were sorted out for the race. It seemed that each time Michael and the Benetton team had to pull out all the stops to turn Friday's poorly-handling Benetton into a winner on Sunday.

A weight problem

At the Brazilian Grand Prix controversy flared up again. When the drivers were weighed at the start of the season Michael topped the scales at 77 kgs, eight more than the previous year. The regs had changed and now the car-driver combination was weighed rather than just the car. *"It's normal that I've put on a few kilos,"* was how he justified himself. *"as my weight is no longer important, I've worked on my muscles."* It was hardly convincing. In the paddock Patrick Head, the Williams chief engineer, calculated that an increase of eight kilos represen-ted 0.2 seconds per lap around the Interlagos circuit; some fourteen seconds over a grand prix.

5 kilos of drink

The Brazilian stewards weighed the driver again at the end of the race - which was not foreseen by the rules - and he was now 71.5 kilos. Michael gave a vague explanation that the difference came from his food and what he drank and sweated out during the grand prix. For the rest of the season the stewards took the second weight into account. It was obvious that the German had tried to stretch the regs to their limit, probably by stuffing his pockets and drinking the maximum amount of water possible before the first weigh-in as had many other drivers including Gerhard Beger and Heinz-Harald Frentzen!

But the flames of controversy burned even brighter at the end of the race. On the face of it Michael had won (Damon Hill had crashed when following the German) from David Coulthard in the second Williams and Berger's Ferrari. A few hours later the first two were disqualified and Berger inherited victory. It was after eight in the evening and Gerhard and Jean Todt, the Ferrari team manager, had waited at the circuit for the Stewards' decision. After hearing the result the whole Ferrari team was over the moon!

Williams and Benetton were supplied by Elf and the Stewards reproached the French petrol company for having provided the teams with fuel which did not conform to the sample that had been sent in at the start of the season as in 1995, no fuel development was allowed. It was a difference in the analysis of this fuel that led to the disqualification of the first two finishers.

Points to the drivers but not the teams

Elf naturally advised the teams to lodge an appeal accusing the Brazilian scrutineers of not knowing how to carry out the analysis and being unable to recognise the identical finger prints. *"We knew that the FIA were after us and we were pretty sure that we would be checked in Brazil,"* said an Elf spokesman. *"But there was no way we'd do anything wrong here."* Several weeks later the counter-check confirmed the discrepancy between the fingerprint lodged and the fuel used and the FIA Appeal Court decided that the drivers should retain their points reckoning that they derived no advantage from the difference. Gerhard Berger was thus a symbolic winner for a few days. The teams, however, did not recoup their points and were fined 200 000 dollars. It was yet another incident that Formula 1 could well have done without.

The fright of his life

After his Brazil win Schumacher went to an island off Salvador de Bahia with his manger Willy Weber and Corinna his girl-friend later to become his wife in August of the same year. Michael and his trainer Harry Hawelka went off for around 30 minutes deep sea diving while Willy and Corinna stayed on the boat and went to sleep.

When they awoke some 45 minutes later there was nobody to be seen. The boat had drifted and it was impossible to see the divers who had resurfaced, because of waves that were over one metre high. Michael had to swim for more than an hour to rejoin them. *"It was the worst moment of my life,"* said the German at the Argentinean Grand Prix; *"I was scared to death. When I resurfaced there was nobody and no boat. Later on I saw it but they didn't see me. Finally, I got rid of my bottles and my life jacket to be able to swim more quickly."* Michael was completely exhausted when he clambered aboard the boat. That day he owed his survival to his exceptional physical fitness.

Programme difficulties

He could do no better than third in the Argentinean Grand Prix. The marriage between the Renault engine and the Benetton chassis proved more difficult than expected because the British team had to adapt its methods and engine management systems to those of the French manufacturer, something which Williams had been doing for ages.

At Imola Michael was on pole which was a big surprise for him as during private testing on the Jerez circuit the Benetton was a good second slower per lap than the Williams. In the race he was leading until he went off in a big way on the eleventh lap. *"After my tyre change the car became very unstable. I don't know what happened but I suddenly lost it."* It was the heaviest impact of his whole career and he was lucky to get out without a scratch. In the championship he was second six points behind Damon Hill, the Imola winner.

Next up was the Spanish Grand Prix. On the Friday Michael described the B195 as the worst car he had ever driven. On Saturday he still managed to claim pole some six-tenths of a second ahead of the field. *"Yesterday the car was terrible but because I was not too far down the time sheets I thought I could pull a rabbit out of the hat today. We changed all the settings and the handling came back,"* he explained on Saturday. In fact, there were two completely different ways of setting up the B195, one of which worked on some circuits and not on others. The team tried to foresee what type of setting suited which circuit but often went the wrong way. This explains the huge gap between the times set by Michael on Friday and on Saturday. He completely dominated the Spanish Grand Prix on the Catalunya circuit which was one of the most boring races of the season.

In Monaco the Benetton driver came off best. Damon Hill, who had set pole, chose the wrong refuelling strategy and Michael took advantage of it to pass him during pit stops. He won again and was now 5 points ahead of the Englishman.

In Canada Schumacher was leading the race until his Benetton retired with electrical problems eleven laps from the end. In Magny-Cours he was back on the top step of the rostrum winning comfortably from Hill and it seemed that the latter's chances of the title were on the wane.

Robot or human being

But Hill was not about to give up so easily. At Silverstone a few days before the race the Englishman launched a blistering verbal attack against his rival. *"Today, the sponsors manufacture every aspect of a champion. Michael Schumacher is a good example. The Mercedes people taught him how to drive. Michael is not a human but a robot, a manufactured product."*

The German hit back through the press by saying that Hill was only the no.1 Williams driver thanks to Senna's death and he didn't deserve to win the championship. In Magny-Cours Michael had accused the Brit of braking on the straight to hinder him when he was following the Williams: a practice completely forbidden in motor racing. "Now I know what kind of man Damon Hill is," thundered the German. "The next time he does the same thing to me I'll know what to do!"

Suicide attack

In the race the animosity between the two men went up a notch as they collided: the Benetton had got past the Williams thanks to refuelling - always done more quickly by Benetton than Williams - and Hill wanted to take advantage of his new tyres to get back in front. He made a suicidal attack and both cars ended up in the gravel trap. Michael, however, was still eleven points ahead in the championship.

Then came Schumacher's home grand prix on the Hockenheim circuit. Pole sitter was Damon Hill but on the second lap he went off leaving the way open for Michael to win his national grand prix, the first time ever by a German in the history of F1. The 128 000 spectators in the Hockenheim stands and tribunes were in a trance. *"What I feel today is just unbelievable,"* said Schumacher. *"I feel even more joy than when I won my first championship title."*

In the Hungarian Grand Prix Hill tried to make up for his two blunders at Silverstone and Hockenheim to belie the nickname Benny Hill which the German spectators had christened him on banners displayed at the circuit.

Mission accomplished. The Englishman was unbeatable in both practice and the race. Michael, who ended up third quickest, was blocked behind David Coulthard's Williams for a long time. He then had to make two consecutive pit stops as his team didn't manage to fill the tank during his first one. Finally, he retired four laps from the end when lying second and Damon Hill pulled back another ten points reducing the gap to eleven.

Marriage with Ferrari

The Hungarian Grand Prix was another turning point in Michael's career as it was here that he announced his arrival at Ferrari in 1996 for whom he had signed a week previously in the utmost secrecy - two weeks before at Hockenheim he had said that this 'marriage would not take place until the autumn'. This announcement hit the headlines and sparked off a whole raft of driver changes in its wake (see chapter 6).

The Belgian Grand Prix two weeks later was the craziest race of the season due to typical Ardennes weather which alternated sun and rain. The duel between Michael and Damon Hill was awesome as they overtook each other no fewer than five times! Once again the Benetton driver came out on top as he stayed out on dry tyres on a soaking wet track and fought off the Williams shod with rain rubber. Result: first Schumacher, second Hill.

At Monza the pundits said that the championship was over as Michael had fifteen points in hand over his rivals none of whom looked capable of beating him.

Another collision

Damon Hill, though, was not prepared to throw in the towel. On the 24th lap of the race he was in third place behind Schumacher and in the Seconda Variante chicane he missed his braking and hit the Benetton up the rear. *"I turned into the corner normally. Suddenly I felt a big bang as Damon hit me. It was not a slight impact - he really crashed into me. It's the second time he's done that this season but he won't admit he's wrong. I've had enough..."*

Estoril was another disappointment for Hill who finished third. Michael finished second behind Coulthard and was now seventeen points ahead of the Englishman with four races left to go: the latter admitted that now only a miracle could win him the title. It didn't happen as he crashed out in the rain in the European Grand Prix won by Schumacher.

The youngest ever double champion

Michael then won the Pacific Grand Prix on the Aïda circuit giving him his second world championship. *"It's a strange feeling for the moment; everything was so tense during this race that I don't yet feel the joy of winning the title."* He was strangely calm when he stepped down from the rostrum almost as though he did not understand what had happened to him.

Nonetheless after a battle with Damon Hill that lasted fifteen grands prix Schumacher became the youngest driver ever to win the world title two years running.

In 1994 his victory had been spoiled by controversy but in 1995 he showed that he was the master. On the Aïda circuit where a fourth place would have been enough to give him the title he showed his competitiveness by winning the race while Hill, who had to win to keep his championship hopes alive, came home third.

Once again the Williams team's strategy had shown its defects whereas Benetton had planned the refuelling stops perfectly: *"I have to admit that the way in which these stops were carried out was simply unbelievable. I've never seen anything so perfect."* Schumacher commented.

Encouraged by his second title the German prepared to join Ferrari, a departure that Flavio Briatore regretted bitterly. *"We're losing something with Michael Schumacher's departure but he's losing something too,"* snapped the Italian at Aïda. *"At least that will allow someone else to win the title next year. You've got to have change in life...!"*

At Suzuka a week later Michael scored his ninth victory of the season (equalling Mansell's 1992 record) in torrential rain thus assuring Benetton of the Constructor's title. All the pre-season aims had been achieved.

Arrival of the red tornado

Michael Schumacher has never been afraid of a challenge. The Renault-powered Benetton was the class of the field thanks to an engine that was simply the best thus making winning a lot easier.

Even before his second world championship title Michael had signed a contract with Ferrari for the 1996 and 97 seasons. Which caused a few eruptions in the little world of Formula 1. *"I really don't understand him,"* exclaimed Bernard Dudot, the Renault chief engineer on the eve of the Hungarian Grand Prix. *"We've again proved yet again that our engine is the best and that the Ferraris finish a lap behind - when they finish!- With us he could have won the championship again. I just don't get it."*

No to Williams

Bernard's surprise was shared by many observers. For Michael, however, his transfer to Ferrari was the only worthwhile way of continuing a career that was about to be enhanced by a second title. *"I could have driven for Williams,"* the German said later. *"I received an offer and all I had to do was up my price to join them. I could've become world champion again but what's the challenge in winning with the best car of the field? I'd been with Benetton for four-and-a-half years. I'd had some great times and a lot of success. I'd achieved all my aims and I felt that I could no longer progress with them. I was looking for a new challenge, a fresh motivation, a new way of evolving. I love real racing which for me means battling for victory. I really had to fight for my success in 1995; none was easy. If I compare my nine wins with those of Nigel Mansell in 1992 I saw that on several occasions he'd won by over a lap which wasn't my case. They were all difficult which makes them all the more rewarding."*

Petrol money

The challenge was Ferrari, a team that had not won the world championship since Jody Scheckter's title in 1979. It proved to be a huge one and infinitely more complex than Michael had anticipated as it took him five years to be crowned for the third time.

Thanks to Shell replacing Agip as the Scuderia's fuel supplier the company was able to pay the 25 million dollars demanded by the German and so the contract was signed. *"Money is important; it's obvious,"* said Schumacher *"but it wasn't the most important thing as another team offered me more."* It was probably McLaren whose engine supplier Mercedes-Benz was ready to stop at nothing to sign Michael.

His entourage was completely in favour of him signing for the Scuderia. As Willy Weber commented in his usual direct style: *"it was an opportunity for him to become more famous than the pope!"*

It was very important for Ferrari to have signed the young German. The Scuderia had gone through many lean years which had cost the FIAT Group, its main source of finance, a lot of money. Results and world titles were needed and this required the best driver. In Italy the feeling was that if Ferrari couldn't make it with Schumacher then it couldn't make it at all. He was the best bet and in case of failure then the team would bear the full responsibility. Were he successful then spectators would praise his talent to the skies as he would be the saviour of Ferrari. Thus, signing Michael was a double-edged sword for the Scuderia as it had a lot to gain but also a lot to lose.

Modest objectives

When signing the contract the German was well aware of the difficulties awaiting him at Ferrari. *"I don't think we'll be fighting for the title in 1996: we have to be realistic,"* he warned. *"On the other hand we can maybe do it in 1997. I'll be really very happy if we are competitive and win a few races in the first season. If we win two or three grands prix in 1996 we'll have fulfilled our objectives."* This turned out to be a prophetic comment as Michael won the Spanish, Belgian and Italian races in his first year with Ferrari.

While he managed to finish on the rostrum four times in the first events he had a very difficult summer because of numerous mechanical failures on the Italian cars. *"In 1993, the overall level at Ferrari was really low,"* explained Schumacher. *"Since Jean Todt's arrival many things have evolved. Unfortunately, the team has changed the design of the car each year which makes progress difficult. In 1996, everything was new. The engine was a V10; the chassis was rethought and so of course we ran into fresh problems. In addition, the car was ready very late, just before the start of the season which didn't give me time to sort it out. But I was expecting this kind of difficulty."*

When Michael said that the car was ready late it was a euphemism for a situation which was verging on the edge of catastrophic. At the end of February during the final private practice on the Estoril circuit Ferrari was the major absentee.

Its new single-seaters, the F310s, had only been presented to the press in Italy on 15th February at the end of the previous week. Take the time it took to load them onto the transporters, add two days' travelling and finally three superb red lorries arrived at Estoril for the start of the last week of practice. It was making a mountain out of a molehill as the only treasure on board this armada was a 412T2, a 1995 model.

Michael Schumacher arrived at Estoril at the same time still with his usual smile on the corner of his mouth. *"We ran into a few gearbox problems during the initial shake-down on the Fiorano circuit,"* he explained. *"There was no sense in running the new car without modifying a part in the gearbox. This is why we've only got a hybrid car here fitted with the new V10."*

The problem was the splitter in the gearbox, a part in carbon which had a tendency to crack leading to irremediable gearbox failure due to loss of oil. The new season had got off to a great start!!

The Scuderia's fantastic technical potential was demonstrated as the new splitter designed by John Barnard, the technical director of the era, was finished on the Tuesday evening in England. It was transported to Maranello during the night, fitted on Wednesday and tested at Fiorano by Eddie Irvine. Michael then had to go back and test it in turn and the two drivers arrived back in Portugal on the Friday with the new cars.

Eliminating the faults

The new F310s arrived in Melbourne with just one day's practice to their name and Michael created a big surprise as he was quickest in the first morning practice. *"I'm very satisfied with the F310,"* said he after his first day with Ferrari. *"It's a good basis and the car is making rapid progress and already we're in the same second as the quickest. It must be remembered that we've not been able to carry out any development work. We're now going to get down to sorting out the minor glitches that we're finding but we don't know how many there are. We haven't been able to do any long-distance testing with the new car, and frankly I'll be pretty surprised if I see the chequered flag in the race."*

The double world champion seemed very relaxed and even indulged in a bit of tomfoolery with the photographers who were snapping him. He gave the impression of really having fun at the start of the 1996 season. *"I'm doing my work without any feeling of pressure as I'm sure that we will resolve all the problems. That'll take at least three or four races and it'll probably be too late to think about winning the championship. Too bad! I'm not a dreamer and I prefer to set myself a realistic goal, winning two or three races. I've always been somebody who's played down his chances. This way at the end of the season everybody is happy if things have gone better. I don't see any need to change this philosophy."*

Rapid adaptation

Michael quickly adapted himself to his new universe and to a car that was completely different from the Benetton he was used to driving. *"When the car isn't easy to drive like the F310 in 1996 sometimes you have to fight very hard to be quick. I must admit that I got a certain kick out of struggling to improve a car that wasn't very competitive,"* he said later.

The season was full of ups and downs but turned out to be less disastrous than initially feared. After a relatively promising start the Ferrari team went through a very lean patch during the summer before things looked up. For the Scuderia 1996 marked not only the arrival of Michael Schumacher in the squad but also the launch of the V10 engine a radical philosophical departure from the V12 used for so many years.

A brief overview of the season

During practice for the first grand prix in Melbourne Michael was beaten by his team-mate, Irishman, Eddie Irvine. The German explained that he had put too much braking on the rear of the car and had not been able to go any quicker. In the race he soon overtook Irvine and was the only one able to match the pace of the two Williams. Finally, he retired on lap 33 having shown to most people's surprise that the Ferrari was competitive in spite of its complete lack of development. It was a promising start.

This positive impression was not destined to last; A few days after the return from Australia the Scuderia grafted the rear of the 1995 car onto the F310 which was still suffering from serious gearbox problems. Michael finished third in the Brazilian Grand Prix on the Interlagos circuit but it was a flattering result that masked major problems. *"I think that I was losing out to the quickest in all the corners,"* complained the German. *"Everything still has to be done on this car. That's what makes me feel optimistic; I know that we can improve in all areas, suspension, the V10 engine and the aerodynamics."*

Steeplechasing!

In Argentina a week later Schumacher managed to qualify on the front row while Eddie Irvine could do no better than tenth. *"I don't know how Michael succeeds in getting anything out of this car,"* muttered the Irishman. *"It's completely undriveable over the bumps. It jumps so much that I can't keep my feet flat on the pedals on the straight. Since the team changed the rear end it's catastrophic."*

In the race the Irishman finished fifth while the German retired after being in second place for a long time.

When the Scuderia got back from South America it began burning the midnight oil to improve the reliability of its cars. This helped Michael to finish second in the European Grand Prix on the Nürburgring circuit after having spent most of the race harrying the winner Jacques Villeneuve in his Williams. *"We know exactly what has to be changed to be competitive but don't expect us to win too soon as we've still got a lot of problems. I'm confident, though, and by mid-season we should be in with a chance."*

At Imola for the following grand prix Schumacher set an unexpected pole position and notched up another second place. In Monaco he again set pole in his F310 but on the first lap in the wet he made one of his rare errors and hit the guardrail at Portier.

A memorable victory

It was a different story in the following race, the Spanish Grand Prix. Here in monsoon conditions Michael did not make any mistakes and scored one of the greatest wins of his career and one that has become part of racing legend. He messed up his start and rounded the first corner in tenth place but by lap 12 he was in the lead after which he opened up a huge gap over his pursuers at around four seconds a lap! And so he won his first grand prix for Ferrari in dreadful conditions: *"This circuit is really not made for rain,"* he stated. *"There were rivers running across the track which moved according to the violence of the showers. This is without taking into account the standing water that made some places incredibly tricky. I lost control of the car on several occasions. What was worst of all was the cold! I was soaked and I froze in the cockpit. I must ask Ferrari to install central heating for the next time!"*

The Scuderia celebrated this victory in the style it deserved. Their joy was short-lived as their lean summer months were about to start. In Montreal Schumacher's V10 refused to fire up for the formation lap and he had to start from the back of the grid. He then found that his car was undriveable and retired with a transmission problem as a part of the rear drive shaft had broken after refuelling.

White smoke: black day

It was even worse at Magny-Cours even though Michael qualified on pole with Eddie Irvine back in tenth place. He was losing half-a-second to his team-mate in the Adelaide corner alone. He was then disqualified as his barge boards were 15 mm too high.

In the race Schumacher was unable to take advantage of his pole position as his engine blew up on the formation lap. *"On the spot I was furious as all the work we'd done in practice went up in smoke. But I calmed down quickly as you've got to know how to control your feelings in such circumstances. I knew that I'd have reliability problems when I signed with Ferrari but I thought that they'd be solved after the start of the season. There's no time for despair.*

You've got to get in there and get on with it." For Jean Todt, the Ferrari team manger, *"it was the worst day of his life."*

And two weeks later in England things didn't improve as Schumacher, who qualified on the second row because of a lack of grip, went out on the third lap with a blocked gearbox. After analysing the problem it was discovered that a 40 centimes bolt that had caused the breakdown. Eddie Irvine in the other Ferrari managed two laps more before breaking his differential.

There was uproar in the Ferrari camp. The Italian press was full of vitriolic attacks on the Scuderia and Jean Todt saying they wanted his head and he answered that if the management wanted it they could have it! Michael was the first to defend his team manger while John Barnard, the car's designer didn't know what to do anymore. *"We did a lot of endurance testing at Monza without meeting the slightest problems. I just don't understand it,"* he lamented.

Quality in question

The expected fight back began on the Hockenheim circuit. The Scuderia had had a clean out in its quality control department and named Gambini an engineer up to then in charge of quality for the Ferrari touring cars, as chief. In the race Michael saw the chequered flag for the first time since his Spanish win finishing fourth.

In Hungary the German proved that the team was competitive again by qualifying on pole on a circuit which is not very demanding on the chassis (a bit like Monaco). In the race he led for 19 laps before beginning to lose ground because of throttle linkage problems. *"It wasn't easy. The throttle was wide open and I had to cut the engine with the emergency switch before the corners and then restart it."* He ended up by getting his hands all crossed up and seven laps from the end activated the circuit breaker. The car refused to restart. *"I'm not frustrated,"* he said repeating the refrain already uttered more than once. *"I didn't expect to fight for the title in 1996. I'd prefer to have all the problems this year rather than next."*

Spa to the rescue

In Belgium the German had a very big accident in Friday's practice which resulted in severe bruising above his right knee. On Saturday he qualified in third place and won the race on Sunday after a very intelligent refuelling strategy. Following Jos Verstappen's huge accident in his Arrows, the safety car took to the track to neutralise the race. Michael took advantage of this to refuel immediately while the two Williams drivers stayed out a lap too long. And so he won his first race in the dry for Ferrari. But it wasn't that easy. *"My steering began to loosen. I almost stopped in the pits to retire but my engineers assured me by radio that it wouldn't break. I continued but it didn't make Eau Rouge any easier!"*

Monza: red flood

It was Italian Grand Prix time. Following the Spa win the royal park was swarming with Tifosi. On Friday Michael fulfilled the Tifosi's hopes by setting the fastest time, a feat that he failed to repeat on Saturday due to a headwind on the straight from which the Ferraris suffered more than the other cars. Well, that's how Michael explained it anyway!

In the race everything went well for the German as he scored a magnificent win. Getting off to a slow start (he finished the first lap in sixth place) he took advantage of the retirements of cars in front and a well thought-out refuelling strategy to go into the lead on lap 31 where he stayed until the finish.

Tifosi against the national anthem

Monza went crazy when he appeared on the rostrum. Such madness had never been seen before in the memory of the Tifosi. *"It was awesome, crazy, completely crazy,"* was how Michael described it. *"Never in my life have I felt such emotions on a rostrum. The Tifosi were screaming so loudly they drowned out the national anthems."* The German was at a loss to describe his feelings following this victory.

It was the high point of the year for Ferrari as the end of the season was more difficult. In Portugal he finished fourth without ever being in a position to battle with the Williams. In Japan, the last race of the season, he came home second behind Damon Hill who succeeded him as world champion.

Aims achieved

A nerve-wracking season came to an end on Japanese soil. The German had not won the championship but he again proved that he was the class of the field as he owed his three victories to his talent and determination thus achieving the aims haphazardly fixed before the start of the year.

The Scuderia began working on the 1997 car in the summer of 1996: *"I now see exactly what the fundamental problems of the F310 are,"* said Michael at the time. *"We can't change them this year given the time we have left. Next season should be a lot better and we should make progress staying with the same overall design, keeping what works and changing what doesn't. In my opinion Ferrari will show its true potential in 1998. That's why I'm negotiating extending my contract until then. Afterwards we'll see."*

Large sums involved

On 5th November the bells of Maranello rang out at last. After several weeks of hard negotiations the Scuderia and Michael Schumacher had reached agreement to pursue their collaboration for another two years, 1998 and 1999.

The previous week Giovanni Agnelli, one of the key directors of the FIAT group had expressed his desire to see the contract with Schumacher extended insisting on how much the German had contributed to the revival of the Scuderia.

It was apparently on the salary asked for by Michael - some 30 million dollars - that the negotiations stalled. At first Luca Di Montezemolo, the Ferrari President, was not prepared to fork out such a large sum. Schumacher at this stage of negotiations was not in the strongest of positions as he admitted himself. He knew that he had to stay at Ferrari if he didn't want to see someone else take advantage of all the hard work he had invested to put the Scuderia back in victory lane.

Neither did the Ferrari directors have a lot of room for manoeuvre: they could not let Michael go to another team - Williams for example - in 1998 while the German had announced in public that his priority was to drive for Ferrari. The Tifosi and the FIAT Group would certainly not have pardoned the Scuderia had they let him escape thus the words uttered by Agnelli were a warning signal to Montezemolo. As if by magic an agreement was quickly found and Schumacher could concentrate completely on the 1997 championship with a clear mind.

Steve Domenjoz

CHAPTER 7

1997 – 1999: Two taxing years

The 1997 Ferrari, the F310B was only an evolution of the 1996 car. As Michael explained it was a question of keeping what worked on the F310 and changing what didn't. John Barnard was still the team's technical director.

The year got off to a great start for the German with the birth of his daughter Gina Maria on 20th February 1997, and it was a very confident Michael Schumacher who awaited the start of the season with every reason for optimism.

As always the same refrain came out of Maranello during the winter. In January 1997 the President Luca Di Montezemolo had asserted that this year for sure Ferrari was aiming for the world title. Jean Todt was more circumspect and hoped that the Scuderia would win more races than in 1996.

Optimistic forecast

On paper anyway Luca Di Montezemolo had every reason to hope. The new F310B was ready at the very beginning of January thus the Scuderia had enough time to improve the set-up and reliability both areas which had let the team down in 1996. In 1997, it looked as if they had finally got the car right.

After the first tests it was obvious that this was far from being the case. Straight off the F310B was crippled by front end problems, a big handicap in tackling fast corners. After a week of private testing on the Estoril circuit the team's morale was at a low ebb: *"It's not this year that I'll have a car capable of winning the world championship,"* complained Michael. *"Of course, we've made some progress in the past few days. The new car is better than the 1996 model; it's faster and*

easier to drive. But I don't think that's enough to win the championship. Don't count on seeing me on the rostrum in Melbourne."

In Maranello the depressing conclusions of the first shakedown test had the effect of a bomb. A few days later some new suspension parts brought some improvements enabling Michael to beat the Fiorano circuit record held by the previous year's car. *"I think we've found a few solutions,"* he admitted tentatively.

Changes at the top

Then behind the scenes Ferrari separated from its technical director, John Barnard, whose contract did not end a priori until July. This was bad news for the Tifosi as it was going to be difficult for the team to develop the F310B without its designer

However, the divorce between the Scuderia and its quirky, problematic engineer had been on the cards for several weeks. The Englishman with his increasingly extravagant demands and the Italians with their cautious budgetary approach no longer saw eye to eye. The latter had up till then accepted all Barnard's caprices - even building him a technical centre in Guilford - as the Englishman had refused to move to Italy. This refusal was one of the main stumbling blocks between the two parties. Ferrari wanted to concentrate all its forces at Maranello to improve efficiency and had come up against Barnard's refusal to bring the Guilford centre to Italy. Thus, the Scuderia ended its collaboration with a man who had been recalled in 1993 at top dollar.

Holidays over

On 17th February Rory Byrne, a South African designer, took over. He had been with Benetton for over 15 years and had decided to retire at the end of the previous season to enjoy a carefree life on an island near the Thailand coast. Jean Todt certainly had to employ all his diplomatic skills - and no doubt economic ones as well - to coax him back to the drawing board.

At Ferrari Rory met up with his old mate, Michael Schumacher, with whom he'd won the 1994 and 95 world championhips at Benetton and another familiar face from the knitwear team, Ross Brawn, named technical director and entrusted with overseeing the technical organisation of the Scuderia.

He had been taken on by Ferrari on the express request of Michael himself. Up till then the post of technical director had been filled by Jean Todt who did not really have either the competence or the availability as he admitted himself.

Brawn brought his calm, methodical way of doing things to Ferrari which had already worked wonders at Benetton. *"With Benetton if practice began at nine o'clock someone came to get me in the motor home at five to,"* remembers Schumacher. *"At Ferrari it was time for another Cappuccino!"*

Praise for a driver

If the German was delighted at the prospect of working with Ross again the pleasure was mutual. *"The main thing that comes out of collaborating with Michael is his implacable logic,"* he explained. *"He's able to analyse the behaviour of a car corner by corner and provide all this information with suggestions as to how to improve the situation. With him each set-up change inevitably makes him go quicker. Of course, the telemetry gives us a lot of data but when it comes to improving the car, we trust in the driver's sensations. For example, the telemetry informs us that the car is under-steering in a corner or on the exit of a corner but it's Michael who tells us which of these problems is costing him the most time."*

Master class

Ross Brawn found that Schumacher had changed since his Benetton days. *"It seems to me that he has become more independent. This is certainly because Ferrari involves its drivers more deeply in the development of the car than we did at Benetton. Michael, though, is without doubt the best driver I've ever worked with. I never had the opportunity of working with Ayrton Senna or Alain Prost but Michael's in the same class."*

The German found that Brawn's arrival more than compensated for Barnard's departure: *"Now development is in one place instead of two. In my opinion Ross will have a considerable influence on the future of Ferrari. It's already apparent where working methods are concerned. He's very logical and well-organised. Today the structure and the people are in place."*

Lost before the lights go out

There was no doubt that for 1998 this team was going to build an excellent car but there was still 1997 to get through. At the very start of the year after the initial difficulties in testing the F310B it seemed that Michael had already written off his chances in the championship. For once in his career he was wrong.

The Australian Grand Prix was the season's curtain raiser. The German qualified third, not bad for a driver who claimed he expected only a few points from this race. He finished second behind David Coulthard's McLaren which scored an unexpected victory.

Jean Todt, the Ferrari team manger, had a big grin on his face as Michael's second place showed that Ferrari would be a force to be reckoned with in the championship. *"I couldn't have expected anything better,"* admitted the Frenchman. *"These six points provide an excellent start to the season."*

The second grand prix was in Brazil and Michael's front row position in qualifying flattered only to deceive as in the race he was unable to match the pace of the Williams and Benettons and finished an anonymous fifth.

Too slow on the straight

The car's top speed was too low. It was one of the main defects of the F310B's chassis as in practice the German was giving away 6 km/h to the Williams at the end of the straight. *"Frankly, I was hoping for better than fifth but the two points scored today could be useful at the end of the year. We've got a traction problem. In addition, as I expected even stopping twice my tyres didn't last the distance."*

The Ferraris were outclassed by the Williams and Benettons and in certain conditions by the Prosts and McLarens and getting back on the winning track seemed a distant prospect. A large number of sleepless nights looked on the cards in Maranello all the more so as nothing could really be modified before the Argentinean Grand Prix two weeks later because all the cars stayed in South America between the two events.

The Argentinean race was one to forget for Schumacher. He qualified fourth on the grid and was eliminated in a first corner accident.

Persevere with the car

After three grands prix the situation was far from brilliant and the outlook for the rest of the season was pretty grim. *"Our potential is better than last year,"* said the German. *"We have to find a solution to our problems and make do with the car. There's no question of throwing it away and building a new one. If we don't manage to improve it'll just be another wasted season and I'll wait for next year."*

For Michael the F310B's main problem was balance. *"To go quickly an F1 car must race with the front and rear wings at the minimum angle. If it's very twitchy in the corner then we have to find grip by loading the wings which penalises straight line speed. The Williams manages to combine grip and top speed."*

However, at Imola in the following race the Ferraris began to improve. Traditionally, the circuit helps the red cars as the Maranello factory is not too far away and the team does a lot of testing there. Also its particular layout - straights broken up by chicanes - favours engines that have good torque and the track is not particularly demanding on chassis.

In practice Michael qualified third thanks to the new 046/2 engine used for the first time that Saturday and the next day both Schumacher and Irvine finished on the rostrum. Never had the Scuderia been so close to matching the performance of the Williams.

The Tifosi did not see things in that light. For them the race was one to forget even if both drivers were on the rostrum as the only thing that counted was victory.

A fantastic car

On the other hand the San Marino Grand Prix result gave Michael Schumacher's morale a tremendous boost as for the first time that season the Ferraris were able to match the pace of the Williams. He hadn't won but he was just a few car lengths away from the victorious FW19. Success was in the offing: *"I never thought I'd come second,"* he admitted after the race. *"Given our performance in practice I aspired to a third place at best. I have to say that the car was absolutely fantastic today. It's pretty surprising as we adopted mixed settings in case it began to rain during the race."*

Right from the start the German was glued to Jacques Villeneuve's gearbox and had no problems in following the Williams. *"I was as quick as he was where it mattered on the circuit,"* continued Schumacher. *"We seem to be up to speed which is very encouraging when I think of the improvements in the pipe line."*

Jean Todt shared his driver's enthusiasm: *"It's obvious that we're still a little behind the Williams but we're getting very close. We've got some modifications coming up which should allow us to be in front at the French Grand Prix. What's important is not be left behind in the championship between now and then,"* was how the little Frenchman analysed the situation.

Next up was the Monaco Grand Prix which Michael had already won in 1994-95 and he wanted to make up for his mistake in 1996 (see chapter 6).

And he did. In pouring rain he scored another legendary victory. The Monaco layout is undoubtedly the most difficult of the F1 season. Add rain and it takes on a whole other dimension as the proximity of the guardrails usually means that the slightest error is fatal.

Like Ayrton

By definition exceptional drivers stand out in exceptional circumstances. In 1984, Ayrton Senna made the little world of Formula 1 sit up and take notice on the same circuit in similar conditions.

Michael Schumacher's 1997 win meant that he joined the Brazilian as part of the Monaco Grand Prix legend as well as proving to any remaining sceptics that he was the best of the current F1 drivers.

He was now at the wheel of a Ferrari that was much more competitive than in 1996. Since the start of the season he had consistently stated that he hoped not to get left behind in the title race until the arrival of the new version of the F310B due to appear in June which, he affirmed, would enable to him to battle with the Williams on an equal footing.

In Monaco he was not left behind and to use a biblical metaphor he almost literally walked on water. His victory propelled him into the championship lead and showed that talentwise he deserved a third title.

Fresh as a daisy

The race over Michael parked his Ferrari at the foot of the Prince's lodge, undid his belts and got out of the car. The Monaco Grand Prix winner looked as fresh as a daisy! *"It's true. I feel great"*, he commented a few minutes later. *"Of course, driving in the rain isn't very demanding physically. The steering wheel turns by itself and you're not subjected to the usual lateral acceleration in the corners. It's very easy, in fact!"*

Maybe. But rarely had conditions been so treacherous. After three days' sun rain had fallen in the Principality just half-an-hour before the start which was too late for the organisation of the fifteen minutes' additional practice laid down in the regs to set up the cars for a wet race.

Ferrari had anticipated the problem. With three minutes to go before the pits closed prior to the start Michael changed cars and took the spare. *"We'd prepared one car for dry conditions and another for wet ones. After a lap's reconnaissance I opted for the latter."*

Ten seconds in a lap

It was the right choice as rain fell throughout the race. Once the lights went out the Ferrari vanished into the distance and Michael had a ten-second lead at the end of the first lap! *"Everything went well. In fact, my only problem was between the Mirabeau and Portier corners. I had to let out the clutch in that section as the engine was too powerful for the track conditions. Otherwise I kept up a good rhythm to maintain concentration which was the toughest thing"* commented Schumacher.

And so thanks to this win Michael found himself leading the world championship which boosted his optimism: *"Up to now I've been lucky as the Williams have run into problems. We still have another difficult race, Barcelona. After that I think our chances are good. We'll see."*

That evening Jean Todt promised that the Scuderia would work flat out to bring on the new version of the F310B as soon as possible. And added that the Monaco win was worth more for the team's morale than the 10 points for the championship.

Two weeks later in the Spanish Grand Prix the Ferraris fulfilled the pessimistic words uttered by Michael Schumacher in Monaco. The German found the car very difficult to drive in the fast bends of the Catalan circuit, qualified seventh and finished fourth. He added three points to his total but these were not enough to prevent Jacques Villeneuve, the winner, from retaking the lead in the world championship.

In Canada things went the Ferrari driver's way. He set pole and came home first in a race shortened following Olivier Panis's accident in his Prost.

103 centimetres of sheer happiness

Saturday 14th June 14h00 and the crowd massed in the stands held its breath. The chequered flag had just fallen to end practice but Jacques Villeneuve and Michael Schumacher were still out on the track and everything was possible. The Quebecois crossed the line first without improving but remained first. Then Michael shot out of the last corner in a majestic controlled slide and took the flag. Silence fell. The local hero had been beaten by just 13 thousands of a second! Given the speed at which the cars crossed the line the gap represented 103 centimetres, nothing on a circuit measuring over 4 kilometres. *"I've every reason to be optimistic,"* analysed Schumacher, *"as since the start of the year the car has always been better on full tanks."*

He attributed this pole to the under the skin modifications made to the Ferrari since the Spanish Grand Prix. *"We're giving the chassis a complete overhaul. My chances in this year's championship depend entirely on the efficacy of these modifications. We'll see."*

His victory on Sunday put him back in the lead in the championship and the rest of the season looked promising.

False modesty?

His winning run continued at Magny-Cours although on arriving at the circuit he stated that he did not expect very much from the race. The modifications for his car were not yet ready and the characteristics of the track were close to those of Barcelona which did not suit the F310B. Unless it rained!

Nonetheless on Saturday under a hot sun he was fastest in qualifying. *"I assure you that I'm really surprised to be on pole!"* He was at a bit of a loss to explain how he had managed to out-drive everyone. *"We'll have to analyse the telemetry data to see what happened,"* he said during the post practice press conference. *"But I can't really fathom why the car's going so well. Last week here we had to work very hard to do a 1 mn 15.6 seconds. Today I got round in 1 mn 14.5 seconds. A really unbelievable and inexplicable difference. We put on a new front wing this morning but I don't think that can have such an effect, all the more so as we're still suffering in the first two corners of the track."* He refused to be drawn about the grand prix. *"I don't think we'll have an easy race. I'm even expecting serious problems."*

Ralf against Michael

Heinz-Harald Frentzen sitting beside him was unable to contain himself any longer: *"Michael keeps on repeating that he has to struggle with his car but even so he manages to qualify in front of everybody,"* interjected the Williams driver. *"It's the same for the race; when he says he'll have problems it's a way of taking the pressure off himself and putting it on us."* Ralf Schumacher (third-quickest) continued along the same lines: *"I shouldn't say this as he's my brother but Heinz is right. Michael always tries to play down his chances."*

The Ferrari driver bet on the rain which was probable according to the weather forecast. On Sunday, however, the first sixty laps of the race were run in the dry. This did not prevent him from dominating the event as he opened up a gap right from the start.

The French Grand Prix was a boring procession for most of the event as the intervals between the drivers kept on increasing and Michael built up a big lead with an ease that surprised him. *"I really didn't expect that,"* said an amazed winner after the finish. *"I'd adopted mixed settings in anticipation of the rain which were brilliant in the dry. The new front wing that we've fitted here is wonderful."*

Schumacher used his tightrope walking abilities when the rain finally did fall staying out on slicks and managed to keep his advantage until the chequered flag.

At mid-season he was fourteen points ahead of Jacques Villeneuve while Ferrari thanks to Eddie Irvine's third place was thirteen ahead of Williams in the Constructors' Championship.

Happy anniversary Mr. Todt

Jean Todt was in seventh heaven that evening as he celebrated his fourth year as Ferrari team manager. *"I have to say that I feel a very special sensation today,"* admitted the Frenchman. *"First of all as on arriving here I said to myself that we'd be lucky to finish in the points as our private testing had gone so badly. And secondly, because in looking at the overall situation I see that after four years' struggle without a break we look like we may make it at last. The very fact that we're leading the championship at mid-season makes me appreciate even more the ground covered."*

During the summer of 1997 Michael was frequently reproached about his tendency to underestimate himself. *"But I'm just trying to be realistic,"* he retorted. *"Private testing goes badly and then when we race on the circuit we go quicker. It's unexpected and unpredictable."*

Thanks to Williams

He added that leading the championship was for him a big surprise: *"I didn't honestly expect this. I also owe it to the fact that the Williams haven't scored very often. On the other hand the F310B has behaved like a real racing car since the Canadian Grand Prix. The ambience at Ferrari is hotting up and we're starting to believe in it which creates a dynamic."*

His collaboration with the Scuderia was tops: *"My relations with the team are excellent. I wasn't expecting them to be so close. The engineers rely on my input and have complete trust in me when it comes to technical choices."*

He could have won in England. On lap 39 when he was leading comfortably he had to retire due to a left rear-wheel bearing failure. Six laps later Eddie Irvine also stopped for good with a broken half-shaft.

A breakdown to be celebrated!

Michael did not appear too downhearted when he got out of his car. *"This type of problem can happen; it's racing,"* he said philosophically. *"In fact it's my first mechanical failure of the season. I prefer to look on the bright side today. I was well in the lead when the problem arose which shows that we've now caught up with the Williams. Because of this today is one to be celebrated, not forgotten."*

At Hockenheim two weeks later he did not shine in his home grand prix as he had done at Magny-Cours and Silverstone. The circuit is not that demanding on chassis but the F310B was still suffering from its early season defect, low straight line speed, a major disadvantage on Hockenheim's long straights. Michael did a good damage limitation job by salvaging second place. His main rival Jacques Villeneuve really messed up as he went off into a gravel trap when in fifth place. The German increased his lead in the championship to ten points with seven grands prix still to go.

The Hungarian Grand Prix outside Budapest saw the arrival of the lightened version of the F310B which had shed some 10 kilos, a huge amount in F1. *"We were already down to the minimum weight but losing more kilos allows us to move the masses to lower the centre of gravity,"* explained Jean Todt. This gain helped Michael to pole just ahead of Jacques Villeneuve.

The Canadian got off to a bad start and was fifth at the end of the first lap. It looked bad for him as overtaking is impossible on the tight Hungaroring but a series of problems hit his main rivals and he won the race. He led for only a single lap but it was the one that mattered, the last!

During the Sunday morning warm up Michael went off and bent the monocoque on his race car so he was obliged to drive the spare which he had hardly used in practice and which destroyed its tyres in three or four laps. *"I had to change them three times. We've never met this kind of problem. It's incomprehensible."* He finished in fourth place and saw his rival, Villeneuve, come to within three points of him in the title chase.

(Continued on page 97)

Captions

1995: Simply the best in the rain
Photo: Dominique Leroy

His first win in a Ferrari in the pouring rain in Spain!
Photo: Steve Domenjoz

Spa 1995: Even better on slicks as Michael fights off Damon Hill on rain tyres
Photo: Dominique Leroy

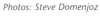

Monaco and Spa 1996: Fighting for those elusive hundredths of a second that make all the difference
Photos: Dominique Leroy

1995 Pacific Grand Prix Aïda: Leaving the pits on the way to another victory
Photo: Dominique Leroy

Spa 1996: Second win in a Ferrari. Michael shares the rostrum joy (and a bottle of champagne!) with Jean Todt
Photos: Steve Domenjoz

Aïda 1995: Flavio Briatore shares the joy of his second world title
Photo: Steve Domenjoz

1996: Last Grand Prix of the year on the Suzuka circuit
Photo: Steve Domenjoz

*(Top) The most sought after cup, the one awarded for the world title
(Bottom) Celebrating with the Benetton team*
Photo: Steve Domenjoz

1996: First Grand Prix of the season in Melbourne
Photo: Steve Domenjoz

1996: A difficult debut with Ferrari but the German still managed to make the rostrum at Interlagos
Photo: Steve Domenjoz

First grand prix with the Scuderia. A pensive Michael Schumacher in the Ferrari pits in Melbourne
Photo: Dominique Leroy

Braking hard for the Ostkurve chicane at Hockenheim
Photo: Steve Domenjoz

(Continued from page 79)

11 second quicker a lap

In Belgium two weeks later it was typical Spa weather, pouring rain, just the type of conditions in which Michael has always been unbeatable. That day, 24th August 1997, he was on another planet. At the start of the race on a soaking wet track he was on intermediates and lapped six seconds quicker than his rivals. The start was given behind the safety car which stopped after three laps. Michael passed Jean Alesi at La Source and half-a-lap later he hustled past Jacques Villeneuve, took the lead and opened up a huge gap. Six seconds at the end of the fifth lap, seventeen on the following one and 1 minute 8 seconds on lap thirteen. His competitors were gob-smacked! At the end of the race even Jacques Villeneuve admitted that the German was the stronger.

He was in fact lucky that it rained. He qualified on the second row and was only 15th fastest in the warm up showing up the limits of the Ferrari on the Belgian helter-skelter. The shower which fell exactly at midday helped him to score another victory. Villeneuve could only finish sixth and Michael's lead in the championship extended to twelve points.

Nothing went right at Monza in front of the Tifosi. The F310B in low downforce trim did not hold the road. At Hockenheim Michael had been able to limit the damage but on the Milan circuit it was a disaster. He qualified on the fifth row and finished sixth. *"Nothing worked,"* he commented. *"Given our problems we can be satisfied with the result as I've lost only one point in relation to Jacques."* The Canadian finished fifth on a circuit that did not suit the Williams either.

A misunderstood penalty

There was a fresh setback on the Spielberg circuit in Austria to which Formula 1 returned for the first time since 1987. Michael was in third place when he was penalised for overtaking Heniz-Harald Frentzen under yellow flags following an accident between Eddie Irvine and Jean Alesi. *"I didn't understand because I didn't see anything. I was close behind Gerhard Berger and I was concentrating on passing him. I didn't see any flags. I was absolutely furious."* He dropped to ninth but really pushed to get back into the points and finished sixth. Jacques Villeneuve won the race and was now only one point behind the German with three races left to run.

At the Nürburgring Villeneuve won again on the German's home territory. All the Canadian had to do was to bide his time until the two McLarens in front of him retired to pick up ten points.

Michael did not score as he was eliminated in the first corner by a collision with his brother, Ralf. This sowed consternation in the Nürburgring stands as the crowd was rooting for Schumacher. Villeneuve now led the Ferrari driver by nine points.

The Scuderia relies on tactics

At Suzuka, the second-last race in the championship it was the opposite. Jacques Villeneuve took pole but was disqualified for not having respected the yellow flags on Saturday morning following Jos Verstappen's accident.

The offence itself did not merit disqualification except that it was Jacques' second offence which, he had been warned, would lead to a one race exclusion. Patrick Head, the Williams technical director, was furious with his driver who should have been more careful knowing the threat that hung over him.

As the Williams team appealed the decision Villeneuve drove in the race while awaiting the FIA Court of Appeal's judgement on his case. Everybody knew that the sanction would be confirmed and the Canadian's decision was pointless. He went into the lead and zigzagged dangerously in front of Schumacher. When the Ferrari rejoined after refuelling Villeneuve tried to close the door on Michael who managed to cut through on the inside. The Scuderia then called upon Eddie Irvine, who was leading, to slot in between the German and the Canadian to slow him down.

Thus Schumacher scored a victory that put him back in the lead of the championship with 78 points against Villeneuve's 77. The last grand prix on the Jerez circuit promised to be a thriller. It was but did not turn out as the German expected!

A heart-stopping show-down

Practice set the tone of the weekend to come. Three drivers all set exactly the same time, 1 mn 21.072 secs, including the two battling for the world championship title Jacques Villeneuve and Michael Schumacher! Suspensewise it was almost too good to be true. In such cases the driver who set the time first is given priority so it was the Canadian who was on pole from the German with Heinz-Harald Frentzen in the other Williams on the second row.

The race lived up to all expectations. No F1 fan could ever remember having experienced such tension during a grand prix. The suspense was at its height in the little press room which was far too small to contain all the journalists who had come to the Jerez circuit for the European Grand Prix.

Michael made the best start followed by Frentzen who let Villeneuve through on the eighth lap.

Up front the two cars were nose to tail and both drivers set almost equal times without either gaining the upper hand in what was an awesome scrap. Villeneuve had to finish in front of Michael and score at least one point to win the title (he had won 7 races and Michael 5 but the German had 78 points and the Canadian 77).

Before the first refuelling stops the German had managed to open up a 5.2 second lead but just afterwards he was held up by Frentzen and Coulthard and Jacques was back on his tail. Then the Canadian in turn was delayed by a Sauber and lost three seconds.

Michael slowed a little after his second stop and Villeneuve speeded up as he found that his car was quicker on new tyres. Within two laps he was all over Schumacher and made a kamikaze attack in the 'Dry Sac' corner. The two cars touched and while the Ferrari ended up in the gravel trap the damaged Williams was able to continue to a third place finish giving Jacques Villeneuve the F1 World Championship title. *"I thought that my passing move had a 50% chance of success,"* explained the Canadian after the race. *"I noticed that my car was much better on new tyres and I had to go for it immediately. It was no good finishing second and I preferred to take the risk of finishing in the gravel trap."*

Kamikaze attack

In fact, after analysis it was clear that Villeneuve's manoeuvre had much less than a 50% chance of success. Maybe 1% would be more exact! Jacques was a second behind on the exit from the previous corner which he tried to make up under braking while Michael explained later that he had left his braking to the very last moment. If he had really thought that the Williams driver was going to try and pass him he would have taken the inside line thus eliminating any danger. The fact that he remained on the outside showed that he was not expecting an attack in this corner.

When he saw the Williams going inside him on the right he turned in brutally to close the door on his rival. It was an ill-timed reflex which was to cost him dearly as he was excluded from the 1997 world championship. It was also one which many other drivers understood: *"I think that all the drivers would have done the same thing in such a situation,"* commented Olivier Panis not known for his aggressiveness. *"You have to understand the situation and the tension that Michael was under. The whole of the Scuderia was counting on him to bring home the title. Hundreds of people wanted it and his was a reflex gesture born out of desperation."*

What Michael did was doubly unfortunate as not only did it led to his convocation by the FIA but it also enabled Jacques Villeneuve to get round the 'Dry Sac' corner. He was for too quick on the entry and would certainly have ended up in the gravel trap if the impact with the Ferrari had not knocked his car to the right and kept it on the track. Had Schumacher got out of the way he could have let the Williams go straight on and stayed in front. In addition, such an impact could have damaged a vital part of the Williams. If Michael had hit a wheel the suspensions would have been bent but the Ferrari struck the FW19 amidships. Jacques Villeneuve said that his car was handling strangely on the straights but that was all.

To sum up, Michael's reaction led to him being accused of dangerous driving but also enabled Villeneuve to stay on the track after his kamikaze attack!

A sanction without consequences

The FIA held an extraordinary general meeting in London on 11th November to decide its position in relation to Michael Schumacher and the events on the Jerez circuit. In the Sunday morning briefing Bernie Ecclestone, the man responsible for promoting F1, had warned the drivers that any dangerous driving would be severely punished.

The rumour doing the rounds was that the FIA would suspend Michael Schumacher for one or more races but that would have devalued the following year's world championship. After hearing the German for over an hour the Council decided to exclude him from the results of the 1997 World Championship allowing him to keep his results and wins but depriving him of his points. Thus, the runner-up spot went to Heinz-Harald Frentzen.

On the other hand no fine or suspension was inflicted on the Ferrari driver who was able to look forward to the 1998 season with serenity. He was simply obliged to take part in several operations in favour of road safety and the fight against road accidents.

It seemed, though, that it was somewhat disproportionate to cancel out the effort invested in 17 grands prix for a driving error. All the more so as the World Council declared that the Jerez incident was the result of a mistake and not a premeditated act. *"His action is no less unacceptable,"* said Max Mosley, the FIA President. *"We wanted to try and find a way of preventing such things from happening again. Suspending him for 1998 would not have achieved our aims."*

The same day Michael Schumacher stated that he was very upset by the decision of the Council: *"It's hard to accept as coming second in the world championship really meant something to me. Well, I made a mistake which I didn't realise until two or three days after the incident. The past two weeks have been very difficult to live through but I accept the sanction. Now I've got to look to the future and I can't wait for the 1998 season to start."*

Ferrari welcomed the Federation's decision with barely disguised relief: *"The decision taken by the Council is hard on Michael,"* commented Jean Todt the Scuderia team manager. *"We respect it and we're going to try and do in 1998 what we were hoping to do in 1997."*

While the German lost his points Ferrari kept theirs and the considerable benefits attached to them. Finally, things did not end too badly for the Prancing Horse as the championship had been lost anyway.

1998: Tyre trouble

On paper anyway the 1998 season looked good. When the new car was presented in front of the brand new Maranello wind tunnel Luca Di Montezemolo was full of enthusiasm. He said that the new car, the F300, was the 'Ferrari of the Renaissance' the one that would at last bring home the world championship.

Nevertheless the first winter tests on the Fiorano and Mugello circuits gave cause for concern. All the more so as in 1998 a new factor came into play: while the Scuderia remained faithful to Goodyear its rival, McLaren, had joined the Bridgestone camp, the Japanese brand having made its F1 in 1997.

In Formula 1 tyres are of vital importance. According to the circuit a tyre can gain or lose a second or more per lap and the fact that the two top teams were with different tyre manufacturers looked like leading to a serious in-balance.

A seven-tenths gap

In Melbourne Michael was third-quickest behind the two McLarens but seven-tenths of a second slower than Mika Häkkinen. He blamed this gap on the tyres: *"We know that our Goodyears are just a tad below the Bridgestones for the moment. We really have to progress in this area if we want to win grands prix."* This was to be his constant refrain for the first half of the season. On every possible occasion he put pressure on Goodyear to force the American manufacturer to improve its rubber and at least equal

Bridgestone which the company achieved towards the end of the year.

In the race Michael parked his Ferrari on the grass on lap 6. *"The water temperature began to rise and the engine suddenly let go. It's a pity as we haven't had the slightest problem during the winter."* However, as the first few laps showed that he was able to keep pace with the McLarens he was confident for the rest of the season. He was right but the future would show that the points he lost that day were irretrievable.

In Brazil the two McLarens dominated finishing first and second with Michael third over a minute behind unable to match their scorching pace.

The following week Ferrari did some intensive testing to improve its chassis and Goodyear prepared to supply some new tyres for the Argentinean race in two weeks time.

Revenge in Buenos Aires

Schumacher got his revenge in Buenos Aires. He qualified on the front row alongside David Coulthard (on pole) saying his place was a small miracle. The new front tyres supplied by Goodyear were in part responsible for this improvement.

Michael again screwed up his start in the race but passed Häkkinen on lap two and did the same to Coulthard on lap five. The attack on the Scot was a pretty aggressive one which sent his McLaren skating off onto the grass. *"David was very wide in this corner,"* justified the German. *"i"*

Once in the lead Schumacher managed to open up a big enough gap to be able to refuel once more than his rivals. He pocketed a victory which, two hours earlier, had seemed highly improbable reducing Häkkinen's lead to twelve points.

At Imola the Ferraris were still four-tenths of a second slower in practice than the McLarens. The race wasn't much better. Häkkinen's retirement allowed Schumacher to finish second behind Coulthard but he was never a threat to the Scot. At least he closed the gap between himself and Häkkinen the championship leader.

In Spain two weeks later it was more or less the same story. In practice he was again third quickest behind the McLarens and after a very poor start he got stuck behind Giancarlo Fisichella and Eddie Irvine until refuelling. He finished a worried third as in terms of sheer performance he was way behind the black and silver cars.

Monaco was even worse. Mika Häkkinen again dominated the race and Michael, who could only qualify fourth, had a coming-together with Alexander Wurtz. It was of his few less inspired moves, something he has done from time to time (as he admits himself he generally screws up badly once per season). The collision with the Austrian's Benetton broke a piece of the F300's rear suspension forcing him to make a long pit stop which dropped him down to the bottom of the time sheets. He finally finished tenth and the gap to Häkkinen was now twenty-two points. It all looked pretty rosy for the Finn.

An indelicate gesture

This was without taking into account the ups and downs of motor racing. Michael turned the tide by winning a crazy, incident-packed Canadian Grand Prix in which both McLarens retired. The German, however, was accused of unsportsmanlike behaviour. On the twenty-first lap the race was neutralised by the appearance of the safety car and Michael dived into the pits. Coming back out he did not see Frentzen bearing down on him and forced the Williams driver to take to the grass to avoid an accident causing his retirement. *"I'm really sorry and I would like to apologise to Heinz-Harald,"* said Schumacher. *"On leaving the pits I looked in my rear view mirror and saw nothing. He was in the blind spot."*

A protest forced him to explain himself to the Stewards and unsurprisingly the affair was forgotten. Although victorious Ferrari was still behind McLaren in terms of performance.

Turning the tables

Three weeks later at the French Grand Prix the Scuderia really managed to turn the tables thanks to improved chassis aerodynamics and above all, better tyres from Goodyear.

In practice Michael split the two McLarens and in the race the Scuderia scored its first double since 1990. *"It's a dream, it's a very special day for us,"* concluded Schumacher who was now back to within six points of Mika Häkkinen in the championship chase.

"On Monday, we can wake up and say we've done a good job," said Jean Todt. *"In two races we've pulled back thirty points on the McLarens."*

The wining streak continued at Silverstone helped by the deluge that hit the English circuit. At the start of the race, though, the German made an error as he began with dry settings on a wet track. The intervention of the safety car - due to a heavy shower - enabled him to make up his forty second deficit on Häkkinen and as the track

dried he took advantage of his set-up and won from the Finn.

The latter then came first in Austria and as at the start of the season Michael could do no better than third.

At Hockenheim, the following week he qualified ninth in front of his fans: his worst qualification at the worst moment! Like the previous year's car the F300 was not fast enough on the straight. In the race he came home an anonymous fifth and Mika Häkkinen won the race increasing his championship lead to sixteen points.

In Hungary Michael was back in the groove. Starting behind the McLarens he was slightly quicker on the twisty little circuit but his problem was trying to overtake on a track where even Thierry Boutsen had managed to keep Senna at bay in 1990. Strategy was the answer! Master tactician Ross Brawn, the Scuderia's technical director asked his driver to come in for an extra unplanned stop thanks to which he passed the two McLarens as he was able to run with a very light fuel load setting incredible lap times. *"When I left the pits for the second time; Ross told me I had nineteen laps to open up a twenty-five second gap to Mika. I said I'd do my best.!"*

This win brought Michael to within seven points of the Finn (who finished sixth).

A questionable manoeuvre

The Spa weather ought to have helped the German to another victory. He was well in the lead in the first half of the race and by lap 25 was over thirty seconds ahead of Damon Hill's Jordan. However, when he was about to lap David Coulthard, the latter slowed brutally on the trajectory on the straight. Due to the spray thrown up by the McLaren Michael was totally unable to judge the manoeuvre and hit the Scot's car hard putting an end to his race and a probable win. After crawling back to his pit Michael jumped out of his Ferrari and rushed down to the Mclaren pit to tell Coulthard exactly what he thought of his driving as he felt the Scot had clearly premeditated his move. *"It's clear. David was lapping in 2 mn 11 seconds before I caught him and in 2 mn 16 secs when I was behind him. It wasn't by chance. He lifted off in a place where we're accelerating hard. I wasn't expecting it at all. He's had enough experience to know that in the rain there was no way I could guess he was slowing."*

At Monza two weeks later the two drivers talked it through but without settling their differences. In Italy, however, the Scuderia scored another double. The two McLarens went into the lead but Coulthard soon retired. Michael overtook Häkkinen sending the Tifosi into ecstasy as the Ferrari driver now had the same number of points as the Finn (80).

At the Nürburgring the Ferraris kept up the momentum and filled the front row. In the race the McLarens found some of their early season speed. Mika Häkkinen was unbeatable and second was the best Michael could do.

Four points at Suzuka

When the teams arrived at Suzuka for the final race Mika was four points ahead of Michael.

Schumacher again took pole but to no avail as he stalled at the start of the formation lap due to a transmission problem which obliged him to start at the back of the field. And what a start! After four corners he was thirteenth having passed eight cars in two kilometres! At the end of the fifth lap he was seventh just twelve seconds behind Häkkinen.

He was then blocked behind the Villeneuve-Hill battle and the gap increased but all hope was not lost. It then stabilised before his right-hand rear tyre exploded on the straight. The 1998 world championship was lost and twelve months' hard work and effort went up in smoke in the space of an hour. *"I'd like to congratulate Mika, he deserves his world title,"* said the Ferrari driver. *"I don't think we lost here at Suzuka but rather at the start of the season. I'm not too disappointed as we can be proud of what we've achieved this year. Life continues and we'll go for it next year!"*

A nerve-wracking 1999 season

So it was back to square one. When the F1 circus found itself back in Melbourne it was like a replay of the previous year, McLaren versus Ferrari. The main difference was a big one as Goodyear had withdrawn from F1 and the two teams mentioned above were both on Bridgestones which eliminated the tyre risk factor.

However, exactly like in 1998 Mika Häkkinen set pole from David Coulthard and Michael Schumacher. The German qualified over one second behind the McLarens which was a bad reminder of the start of the previous season when the Ferraris were slower. Michael was pretty angry when he got out of his car: *"I didn't expect such a gap. We'll have to get down to work next week. We don't really know what's the cause of our problem but I'm sure we'll find it. It's far too early to say our season is compromised."*

In the race Michael had a problem with his steering wheel and had to start from the back. By half-distance he was up to fourth and then had a puncture followed by fresh ignition problems linked to his steering wheel. He finished eight and fortunately for him both McLarens retired. In any case he had every reason to be happy as Corinna gave birth to Mick, their second child, on 22nd of March.

Down to work

In Brazil he qualified fourth and finished second behind an uncatchable Häkkinen. *"After Saturday's practice I was really worried for the rest of the season,"* admitted the German after the grand prix. *"But in the race itself we showed that even if we are just a tad slower than the McLarens, the gap isn't too big. We going work hard between now and the next event."*

In 1998, the McLarens' domination had lasted for several races but in 1999 it was much shorter. The next race the San Marino Grand Prix on the Imola circuit was won by Michael Schumacher from David Coulthard with Häkkinen retiring. Victory was again due to a two stop strategy employed by Ferrari without which the Scot would probably have won. *"We took the risk and it paid off and we seem to have caught up with the McLarens. The gap in qualifying and the race was very small so I'm more optimistic for the rest of the season."*

In the streets of Monte Carlo Michael won his fourth Monaco Grand Prix. He lost pole by a tiny margin but made an impeccable get-away and led from start to finish thus increasing his lead in the championship.

"Monaco is a very particular circuit and we know that several other tracks will be less favourable to us," was his analysis. *"It's good to be able to tackle them with a bit of breathing space as we don't have to take unnecessary risks."*

In Spain a fortnight later Michael qualified on the second row and in the race he finished third behind the unbeatable McLarens. He made a poor start and was blocked behind Jacques Villeneuve for twenty-five laps. Once he got past the Canadian he ate into Coulthard's lead but couldn't get past.

The blunder of the year

In Canada Michael set his first pole of the season. Things looked good for Sunday but after leading for half the race he hit the concrete wall on the entrance to the pit straight and retired. *"I was on the wrong line and the tyres picked up dust. It was completely my fault,"* he admitted afterwards. *"I usually make one mistake during the year and I hope it'll be the last this season."*

A shower during qualifying for the French Grand Prix led to an unusual grid line-up which left Michael in sixth place and Mika Häkkinen in fourteenth! The drivers who went out early were at the front. Michael finished in fifth place after leading a race which he described as chaotic for a few laps. *"My radio went on the blink and I tried to communicate with my pit by hand! In addition, I had a gear selection problem. At one moment I could only select first and second for a whole lap."*

His gearbox problems obliged him to stop at his pit to change the steering wheel. *"The new one didn't really improve the situation and the fresh set of tyres was not very good. I don't know why."*

In the championship Häkkinen, who finished second, increased his lead to eight points. It was mid-season and nothing was lost. Or so it seemed.

Silverstone shock

In 1997 and 1998 Michael had missed the title by a whisker. The way in which the 1999 season turned out showed that he probably would have won the F1 World Championship had he not left the track after the Silverstone race had been stopped!

He started from the front row but got away slowly. He was fourth after two corners and then tried to pass his team-mate Eddie Irvine on the inside at Stowe. A few seconds earlier race Control had decided to stop the race to remove Villeneuve and Zanardi's cars which had stalled on the grid.

Heavy impact

Michael Schumacher did not know this. The McLaren drivers had been informed by radio but the Ferrari team waited before telling Michael and Eddie Irvine. The German's attempt to pass Irvine ended in the guardrail. His brakes failed and his F399 shot off the circuit. It was barely slowed by the gravel trap and hit the tyres head-on spearing through them and burying its nose in the guardrail. It was a huge impact.

Michael was fully conscious but was stuck in his car. He was removed with great care and helicoptered to the Northampton general hospital where a broken tibia and fibula on his right leg were diagnosed. *"A clean and tidy break"*, announced Sid Watkins the drivers' doctor laconically.

Schumacher could have had his leg plastered but instead had an operation enabling a metal pin to be fitted as it led to a quicker recovery. It began around 16h00 and lasted two hours. The German went back to Switzerland the next day and spent a few days in a private clinic before going home. It looked like his season was over.

Test put off

A month later during the German Grand Prix he addressed his fans massed in the stands directly by means of the giant screens at the track. While his entourage had announced that it would be several months before he drove again, he said that he was to test his Ferrari on 7th August. If all went well he would race in the Hungarian Grand Prix. His doctors advised him against doing this test and he agreed. The week before the Hungarian race he had another operation to remove the pin in his leg.

He was back in the car for the first time on 20th August at Mugello. He did sixty-five laps and was quicker than Eddie Irvine! *"It's like coming back to work after a long holiday,"* he joked! However, the day after this test he suffered violent pains in his leg which decided him to convalesce for a few weeks more.

At the start of October there was no question of Michael Schumacher driving again that season. A longer than expected recovery meant that he still felt a lot of pain over the bumps and would not able to compete in the last two grands prix.

On 8th October against all expectations he went back on his decision. After three days' intensive testing at Fiorano and Mugello Michael judged his physical condition to have improved a lot. Thus, he decided to race in the Malaysian Grand Prix on Sunday 17th October. Out went Mika Salo his replacement since the Austrian event.

This turn about meant that the German found the F399 much improved in private testing. His return was perhaps conditioned by the fact that he thought he had a car capable of winning the Malaysian race. For him a victory would show that he could have won the world championship had he not had his accident in England.

Officially his return also enabled him to lend Eddie Irvine a helping hand. Rumour has it that he was obliged to come back and race by Luca Di Montezemolo who had telephoned the Schumacher household. His daughter who answered the phone and said, *"Daddy is playing football in the garden!"* Luca saw red and advised his driver to return, pronto!

Winning comeback

In Malaysia Michael dominated. His pole time was over a second quicker than Eddie Irvine and in the race it seemed like he was playing with his rivals letting his team-mate head on to victory while fending off Mika Häkkinen's McLaren.

In the final race in Japan his job was to help his team-mate win the world championship title. Irvine was four points ahead of Häkkinen and Michael had to win to prevent the Finn from being crowned champion. However, he finished second behind the McLaren driver after having fluffed his start and Irvine took the flag in third place losing the title for himself and Ferrari. A win the Constructors' Championship for the first time in sixteen years provided some consolation for the Scuderia.

It is possible that Michael was not too unhappy with this result as he wanted to be the first Ferrari driver to bring home the title to Maranello since Jody Scheckter in 1979. After 1997 and 98 it was the third consecutive setback in the Drivers Championship, but Michael's stunning end of season performance showed that he

Captions

1997: Argentinean Grand Prix. His front wing broken in an accident at the start
Photo: Steve Domenjoz

1997: Monaco and first win of the season
Photo: Steve Domenjoz

1997: The Monaco rostrum
Photo: Steve Domenjoz

1997: The French Grand Prix and Michael jumps into the lead and heads on to another win
Photo: Steve Domenjoz

1998: Heavy braking in the Brazilian Grand Prix in which Michael finished third
Photo: Steve Domenjoz

1998: Complicity with Eddie Irvine with whom there was never a problem
Photos: Steve Domenjoz

1998: British Grand Prix : Rain and victory
Photos: Steve Domenjoz

"Here's the coffee button and this is for Internet." The steering wheel of the 1999 F399 was complicated to say the least!
Photo: Steve Domenjoz

104

CHAPTER 8

Victory at last

In these the years of fatted cows extravagance characterised the F1 teams' new car presentations. At Jaguar and Jordan for example in January 2000 over one thousand people attended sophisticated sound and light shows. At Sauber some 7000 spectators crowded into the Hallenstadion in Zurich for a spectacle that lasted almost two hours.

Ferrari, however, was not lured into such excess. On 7th February at the ceremony in Maranello the three team drivers - Michael Schumacher, Rubens Barrichello and test driver Luca Badoer lifted the veil that covered the car placed centre-stage, the F1 - 2000 an evolution of the 1999 F399. After a few short speeches drivers and engineers left the scene for interviews.

It was a muted ceremony that seemed to lack passion a striking contrast to the myth surrounding Ferrari. *"Each year is difficult and I've learned not to appear too gung ho,"* explained Jean Todt. *"There's not really much reason to be enthusiastic until we see how the car performs. And what the others have done. Only after the Australian Grand Prix will we know if we're competitive or if we still have a lot of work to do to catch up."*

Rory Byrne, the designer of the F1-2000, looked pretty cool, calm and collected and reckoned that the new car was a big step forward. *"The F1-2000 is a direct descendant of the F399,"* he stated. *"Practically all the parts, though, are new. We've improved everything. Above all we've gained in the area of aerodynamics thanks to our new wind tunnel. We've done a lot of work on the transmission, the lubrication and the suspension with carbon springs. We also have a new system which should help us reduce our refuelling time."*

A favourable premonition

A bronzed Michael Schumacher had not a trace of a limp. He was in top form and full of enthusiasm for his fifth year with the Scuderia. *"I saw the new car for the first time yesterday,"* he commented. *"Rubens and I both said we liked the look of it and it should be quick. I know what the engineers were aiming for; I know how it behaves in the wind tunnel but it's only a premonition as we'll have to see how it performs on the track."*

His love of driving was still as strong as ever: *"Just after the accident I though I'd stop immediately. It's normal. In such a case you realise what could happen to you in this job. You're kind of brought back to reality. After a while, though, things fall back into place. In life you always have to respect certain limits. If you don't you die! It's not just true for Formula 1 but for all activities."*

No rush for 'Schumi'

The Scuderia Ferrari had been chasing the title for 21 years in the last three of which it had escaped them in the final race. Was this to be THE year? In spite of the low profile in Maranello the team seemed quietly confident. A priori the new F1-2000 looked the part. It was finer, lighter than its predecessor - which enabled its centre of gravity to be lowered by adding ballast to the bottom - had a more powerful engine and seemed to incorporate all the ingredients for victory.

Even the possibility of problems did not seem to frighten Schumacher. *"I've got a contract with Ferrari until the end of 2002,"* he said smiling. *"I don't know where we'll be next year but if we don't manage to win the title this year, we'll try again in 2001."*

First blood

Melbourne hosted the first grand prix and practice times promised a battle between Ferrari and McLaren. The opening laps followed the script but the silver cars quickly retired leaving the way open for Michael Schumacher. *"It's a pity that Mika didn't make it to the finish,"* pointed out the German. *"I'd have really liked to show everybody just how competitive we are. At the start of the race I could follow him without pushing; I just nursed my tyres from then on."*

Two-zero for Schumacher

In Brazil, Michael was again third in practice and decided on a two-stop strategy while McLaren went for a one-stopper. The Scuderia's option was all the more risky as the red cars were on the second row. Thus to win they had to overtake the McLarens as quickly as possible which Michael did as he passed both MP/4-15s by the end of the first lap. *"Already at the start I could've pushed and got ahead of Mika but I didn't want to take too many risks and in addition he wasn't too keen on letting me through! I liked our little duel as I don't often have the opportunity to have a wheel-to-wheel battle with him and to pass him."*

Once in front the Ferrari driver pulled out a big lead on his Finnish rival thanks to the fact that his car was lighter as he was carrying less fuel, enough for just a third of the race. The German began to lose ground after his first refuelling stop as on lap 23 he was only seven seconds behind but five laps later the gap had stretched to twenty-three seconds. *"It's true I was a bit worried at that moment,"* he admitted. *"My second set of tyres didn't work well. They vibrated a lot and unbalanced the car."*

A few laps later Mika retired leaving the way open again for the Ferrari - apart from a small problem around lap 60: *"We had a little glitch which the team warned me about by radio,"* said the German. *"I don't really know what it was but I had to slow in certain corners. Maybe it wasn't necessary. I had a big lead and didn't want to take any risks."*

Only he...

In fact, his F1-2000 was suffering from an oil circulation problem and to keep on lubricating the engine Michael had to take the corners differently whether they were left or right-handers. A few days after the race one of the Ferrari engineers said that only Schumacher could have won the race with a car in such a bad state.

With two wins in two races he was now well in the lead in the world championship.

Number three!

The Ferraris again defeated their rivals at Imola. But by a whisker as at the end of 305 kilometres Michael was only 1.1 seconds ahead of Häkkinen, a gap that was an apt reflection of the intensity of this grand prix. *"It was terrific,"* he smiled getting out of his car. *"It was sixty-two qualifying laps. I was on the limit everywhere."*

He qualified on the front row and almost lost several places at the start. *"We'll have to analyse what happened. It was a bit like Suzuka last year. The car didn't respond properly."* After zigzagging in front of David Coulthard he slotted into second behind Häkkinen and spent the early part of the race trying to hang on to the Finn. *"It was a real sprint from start to finish. I really had fun,"* said the Ferrari driver after the race.

Michael took over the lead around the time of the second refuelling stops. Mika was the first to pit and Schumacher took advantage of this to lower the lap record several times before his own stop after which he came out in the lead. It was a tactic used many times by the Scuderia which nearly always worked. The Imola crowd was able to give full vent to its joy. *"We didn't need to change strategy during the race,"* he added. *"Everything went as planned. Obviously we didn't know Mika's tactics. We had to guess and we were proved right."*

The last time Michael had won the first three grands prix of the season was in 1994 when he won his first world championship title. A premonition? *"We're going through a good patch but we know how quickly things can change in F1. Twenty-four points in hand over Mika is not good enough to allow us any respite. We'll keep on working."*

A demon start

As Schumacher admitted himself he often ran into difficulties at the start because of problems specific to his Ferrari. In England, however, where he qualified fifth he made no mistakes and got away perfectly, at least in the first few seconds, when the red lights went out. *"I had the choice of aiming for the middle of the field or trying to pass on the grass. Normally, it doesn't pose any problems but due to the rain that had fallen I had wheelspin and I lost momentum. Jenson Button passed me on the inside, Jacques on the outside followed by Ralf. I could've fought back but it'd have been risky."* It was a disastrous start and he finished the first lap in eighth place.

Blocked behind Villeneuve

Michael found himself stuck behind Villeneuve without being able to get by: *"I was at least a second per lap quicker than him but I had more fuel and as his straight-line speed was good there was no hope of getting past. I asked myself how the race would end."*

Only when the Canadian's BAR stopped to refuel on lap 34 did Michael have a clear track ahead of him. *"I really pushed and as the car wasn't too bad I managed to make up some lost time."* He finally finished third and after four grands prix was 20 points ahead of his nearest rival, David Coulthard.

A mechanic in hospital

Michael set his first pole of the season in Spain which was an encouraging sign on a circuit that was known to favour the McLarens. In the race he led for the first two-thirds but it all went wrong during his second refuelling stop.

In fact, the seeds of the problem were sown in the first one. A mistake by the mechanic giving him the sign to go led to the German accelerating away before refuelling was completed. Nigel Stepney, the chief mechanic, was bowled over by the Ferrari's rear wing. He was taken to the circuit hospital where distended ligaments in his left ankle were diagnosed. *"The guy lifted the sign and then lowered it again,"* said Michael afterwards. *"Unfortunately, you can't stop a car accelerating away so easily. I did feel that I had run over something and in my rear-view mirror I saw a mechanic lying on the ground. I asked what had happened over the radio but got no reply."* The nozzle of his Ferrari's fuel tank was slightly damaged in the incident which made his second refuelling stop last longer and allowed Mika Häkkinen to go into the lead.

In any case a slow puncture forced the German to make a third stop which effectively destroyed his race. The result was a fifth place and two meagre points in the championship. *"You can't be lucky every time,"* said he philosophically.

His best day

The European Grand Prix was run in pouring rain. *"I'm very happy for the spectators who've turned out in large numbers in spite of the weather. My victory is a reward for their courage,"* were Michael's words after the race.

A record 147 000 spectators came to the Nürburgring to cheer on their champion who had missed the two German races the previous year. The rain did not bother them as it was largely thanks to a shower that their hero won the event. Mika Häkkinen made a fantastic start from the second row to overtake the two drivers at the front of the grid: *"Mika made an excellent get away and I started a bit more slowly. I could do*

nothing about him. We were so close in the first corner that we touched but without consequences," Michael said after the race.

After taking advantage of the first drops of rain to pass the Finn the Ferrari team adopted a strategy which obliged the German to do the second half of the race without refuelling. He was now 18 points ahead of the McLaren driver in the championship which gave him a little breathing space. *"This was the situation I dreamt about before the season began. Sometimes dreams become reality. We have the advantage this year and we aim to keep it to the end,"* was how Michael summed it up.

Double in Montreal

He racked up his fifth success in Montreal. The German on pole did not leave his rivals any chance and came home an uncontested winner even though he slowed towards the end and finished just ahead of his team-mate Barrichello.

This was his fortieth victory and gave him a 22 point lead over Coulthard. Title prospects looked good. *"I don't even want to think about it,"* retorted Michael. *"Not until I'm mathematically out of danger will I consider myself world champion. I've had enough experience in F1 to know that nothing is sure in advance."*

At Magny-Cours he qualified fifth. *"At the start of the race I was able to control the situation but my tyres went off quicker than those of my rivals,"* he complained. *"And it ended with an engine problem. We have to analyse all that but there's nothing to be done. It's motor racing."* It was also retirement!

A bad race for the Scuderia which yielded only a third place. *"Obviously, it's been a bad weekend for us. The unwritten rule of the 2000 championship is that if we don't win, 'they' will. It's always the same story. We've known since the start of the season that it would be tough. Today's race proves it,"* was how Jean Todt summed it up.

Zonta eliminates Schumacher

Michael qualified fourth in Austria and although he did not make a perfect start he looked all set to come out of the first corner in third place. *"I made a better start but I had no intention of creating an incident with Michael,"* explained Rubens Barrichello after the race. *"Suddenly I felt as if I was being pushed from behind and I went sideways."*

The Brazilian managed to get back onto the track and finished the first lap in eighth place. Others were not so lucky as Schumacher, Jarno Trulli and Giancarlo Fisichella's race stopped there and then. *"I came into the first corner and I was pushed by*

Ricardo Zonta," said Michael on his return to the pits. *"My car spun and I was hit by Trulli. It's as simple as that. I'm obviously very disappointed but that's racing. Ricardo was just a tad optimistic about his braking abilities but I'm sure he didn't do it on purpose. I too have made the odd mistake in the past...!"*

The German just wanted to forget that day as quickly as possible and left the circuit before the end of the race. *"I hope we can remedy the situation at Hockenheim. It's very important,"* he said.

Ruben's Ferrari which survived the pile up on the A1 Ring did not exactly set the track on fire. *"I had a problem with the flat bottom and the road-holding was catastrophic,"* stated the Brazilian. *"After refuelling it was bit better but my car was light years away from its performance on Friday and Saturday. It's really a pity."*

300 metres and out!

Contrary to Michael's wishes Hockenheim was a disaster. His race lasted three hundred metres to the enormous deception of his fans. Like Austria two weeks earlier the German was eliminated in the first corner after being hit up the back by another car. This time the driver responsible was Giancarlo Fisichella who could not avoid the Ferrari. It was a bitter blow for Michael who had scored only once in the last five races. His lead in the championship had melted away. *"It's really a pity to be hit up the rear once again and to be unable to fight. When this kind of thing happens to you twice in a row it's very difficult to accept."*

The 'serie noire' continues

In Hungary he had no problems at the start even if it was touch and go between him and Mika Häkkinen in the first corner with the German pulling over to the right forcing the Finn to use the pit lane exit to avoid a crash as he blasted through. In the early part of the race Michael was able to match the infernal pace set by the McLaren driver so that after 24 laps he was only 7 seconds behind his rival. The gap then increased to 17 seconds after the first refuelling stop and just under 26 after the second one.

Thus, Michael realised that he would not have won the race whatever happened in the first corner. *"Honestly, we were not quick enough today. I really thought I could win this race but it wasn't the case,"* he admitted afterwards.

Things didn't look too bright for the rest of the season as since the Canadian Grand Prix the McLarens seemed inherently quicker than the Ferraris. *"Today, it was golden rather than silver arrows. It's true I'm worried about the rest of the year. If things go on like this then we've got no chance,"* confirmed the German.

While waiting for an improvement Michael Schumacher and Ferrari had just lost the lead in both Drivers and Constructors' Championships to Mika Häkkinen and McLaren. *"Now I'm the hunter and not the hunted but I think I 've got used to this over the past few years. No?"* quipped Michael.

In Belgium two weeks later it was the same scenario with Schumacher qualifying fourth. In the race Mika went sideways briefly allowing the German into first place. But the Finn was in attack mode and as the race entered its closing stages he ate into the Ferrari's lead. Once he got close to Michael he overtook him in a mind-boggling passing manoeuvre just when the German was lapping Ricardo Zonta. *"We weren't quick enough today,"* said Michael. *"If Mika hadn't passed me in that spot he'd have done so a lap later or the one after. There was nothing I could do about it."*

For the Scuderia the situation in the championship was critical as Michael was now six points behind the Finn with just four grands prix left to run. The early season lead had been transformed into a deficit that it was not going to be easy to pull back especially as the MP/4-15s were in sparkling form.

Forza Monza

The Italian Grand Prix saw a significant turn-around which took a lot of pressure off the team. At the start everybody feared an accident in the very tight first chicane but it happened in the one after. The race was neutralised immediately and out came the safety car to allow the marshals to remove the wrecks involved in the pile up and to transport a seriously injured fireman to hospital.

The race was restarted and turned into a long procession. Michael, who was on pole, eked out a lead over Häkkinen. This was a big surprise for everybody including the German! When he left the rostrum he went to the press conference where he burst into tears. He had great difficulty in pulling himself together and explained later that his emotion was due to the particular context of his victory. *"I think everybody can understand why I broke up. We're in Italy in front of spectators who gave me incredible support during the whole race. And we've come back with a bang after several weeks where we were far from being competitive. I can't find the words to express myself but being back on top and back in the title chase is such a relief."*

Always as solid as a rock Michael had never shown his emotions in public before. The fact that he broke up at Monza illustrated the incredible tension that reigned in the Ferrari camp as well as showing that someone often described as a driving machine was also a human being. He came out of it with his stature increased.

Triumph at Indianapolis

The Schumacher/Ferrari winning streak began again at Monza and was not to stop as the German racked up four consecutive wins at the end of the season.

The USA Grand Prix at Indianapolis turned to the advantage of the red cars in the opening laps even though David Coulthard took the lead in the first corner but he had jumped the start losing any hope of victory. The McLaren driver then decided to hold up Schumacher to let Mika Häkkinen get closer. He did this perfectly until Michael pulled off a daring overtaking manoeuvre at the end of the straight. The German was not happy about this. *"That David held me up in the slow section is normal; it's part of the game but he hit my car when I went wide in the corner and that's not on."*

From then his race was like a Sunday afternoon drive - apart from a big scare when he spun four laps from the end. *"I have to admit that I lost concentration. I was thinking about other things but I'd better not say what,"* laughed the German. *"The team asked me to slow down. I was 25 seconds in front of Rubens and I didn't watch out for the grass on the trackside. After this Ross told me to concentrate and I said I'd woken up!"*

This win helped him to an eight point lead over his Finnish rival in the championship chase. *"It's still mathematically open,"* commented Schumacher. *"We're going to stay concentrated until the very end. There's private testing scheduled this week and also between the Japanese and Malaysian Grands Prix. I know that I can finish second twice and win the championship but I have to do it. These cars are prototypes and as we saw with Mika today a problem can hit anybody. It's not over till it's over, that's how I must think!"*

World Champion

Suzuka. After setting pole in practice Michael crossed the finishing line with the world title in his pocket at the end of a perfect race. The whole Ferrari team exploded with joy and tears ran down their cheeks. The mechanics fell into each other's arms on the pit wall. Jean Todt too had a fit of the weepies. Michael was alone in his cockpit and lived his first title for Ferrari in his own way. *"Crossing the finishing line, I felt an explosion of emotion,"* he said when he got left the rostrum.

The German had already won two titles with Benetton but scoring his third in a Ferrari, the Scuderia's first since Jody Scheckter's in 1979, was something he described as really special, unprecedented. *"I can't explain how I feel at this moment. It's like at Monza even though I'm not going to cry this time! The tension will have to fall before I realise what's happened to me. I've already been world champion but not in a Ferrari. The Scuderia's been waiting for this for 21 years so it's much more important than the ones with Benetton."*

The feelings experienced by the whole team at Suzuka were on a par with the work invested to obtain this result. Michael Schumacher had been driving a red car for five years and had missed out on the title two years running.

Now it was in the bag. And how! He had more than earned his success as he had qualified eight times on pole and won eight grands prix to which he added a ninth pole and victory in Malaysia. The Japanese race was of a rare intensity as up front Mika Häkkinen was setting a blistering pace. He had to win to conserve his chances of keeping his crown. Michael went into the lead after his second refuelling stop thanks to a well thought out strategy and when the rain began to fall at the end of the race making the track very tricky he was home and dry.

The party fully lived up to the importance of the result. *"I'd asked the team not to plan anything as I thought it would bring bad luck,"* said Michael, *"but I'm sure we'll improvise something really fantastic."*

That evening the German was the karaoke bar in the Suzuka circuit hotel with his wife Corinna where he met up with Mika Häkkinen and Erica his other half.

Both titles in the bag

After ten days' holidays on a Malaysian island Michael arrived at the Kuala Lumpur circuit in top form. He again qualified on pole - for the fourth time running - and predicted that the race would be a doddle. It was and the Scuderia had no problems wrapping up its second consecutive Constructors' championship.

For McLaren to win it they would have had to score a double while Ferrari notched up only two points. It was mission impossible from the moment the lights went out as Mika jumped the start and received a ten second penalty five laps later. Up front David Coulthard led Schumacher by around five seconds in the early stages of the race. The Scot stopped very early for refuelling and Ferrari played the same trick as at Suzuka with the same success. While David rejoined with a full tank Schumacher really pushed as his car was lighter thanks to a low fuel load. When he stopped in turn he came out of the pits in the lead. All he had to do from then on was to keep Coulthard at bay even though the Scot loomed large in his mirrors. *"I had to push from first to last lap,"* he grinned after the race. *"I didn't have a second to breathe and relax. It's not a problem. The most important thing is that we've won the championship. The whole team had worked very hard to do it and fully deserves its success."*

Legs in the air

Tan Sri Dato Basir bin Ismail, the director of the Kuala Lumpur airport invited the whole Formula 1 world, drivers, mechanics, engineers and journalists to celebrate the end of the season in the hospitality units above the paddock. Little did he know that his invitation would lead to one of the biggest parties ever in F1 history.

All the Ferrari team members wore one of the famous red wigs seen on the rostrum. For the Scuderia the surprise came at 20h00 when Luca Di Montezemolo, the company president, appeared. The Italian had arrived in Kuala Lumpur that morning but stayed in his hotel to watch the race on TV as he was afraid of bringing bad luck to his team. He had come to the last races in 1997-98-99 and each time Ferrari had lost.

Michael really let his hair down and began the horseplay in the evening when he tore the Mercedes Competitions director Norbert Haug's trousers. There then ensued a general fight from which everybody emerged with their trousers in tatters and naked legs. The Vufflens driver had promised a crazy night after the title and he kept his word...!

Captions

1999: The Spanish Grand Prix. The Ferrari; poetry in action
Photo: Steve Domenjoz

San Marino Grand Prix. With Mika Häkkinen gone (retired) Michael is on his way to victory
Photo: Steve Domenjoz

1999: British Grand Prix. The spectacular traces of braking that cost Michael Schumacher the world title
Photo: Steve Domenjoz

1999: The Japanese Grand Prix. Back after missing seven grands prix Michael set two pole positions
Photo: Steve Domenjoz

2000: The German Grand Prix in the Hockenheim forest. The race was won by Rubens Barrichello
Photo: Steve Domenjoz

2000: German Grand Prix. After an incident similar to the one in Austria two weeks earlier Michael was again taken out in the first corner. He has just got out of his car to estimate the damage
Photo: Steve Domenjoz

Suzuka 2000: In the bag! Michael holds his helmet in his hands in the parc fermé
Photo: Thierry Gromik

Two weeks after the Drivers' title Michael won again in Malaysia clinching the Constructors' Championship. And there were more celebrations after the race
Photos: Steve Domenjoz

CHAPTER 9

2001: Confirmation

In 2000, Michael Schumacher ended a twenty-one-year drought for Ferrari by winning the world championship.

So what about 2001? There were a few question marks hanging over the start of the new season especially from a technical point of view: the new regulations required the front wing to be raised and the number of flaps on the rear wing was limited (much more fundamental changes that they appeared on the surface). The tyre situation had also changed with the arrival of a challenger to Bridgestone.

However, despite these unknown factors the year looked like continuing previous trends for budgetary and organisational reasons and being another struggle between F1's deadly rivals McLaren and Ferrari. Williams upset the apple cart somewhat as its drivers scored four wins exactly the same number as McLaren.

After a few early reliability problems the F2001 Ferrari was ready to defend the Scuderia's honour right from the very first race. Michael Schumacher was genuinely optimistic before the start of the season: *"Many people think that I'll be less motivated this year. Nothing could be further from the truth! I was born to race and the fact that I've won another title doesn't change the pleasure that I get from driving a car on the very limit. On the other hand we'll be under a lot less pressure this year and it'll be all the easier for us to go for the title."*

Ferrari, though, was a bit apprehensive about the engine as the completely new 050 block was lighter than the 049 passing under the 100 kilos barrier. Reliability could be affected by such a weight loss. *"Maybe we're going to run into some problems in the early races,"* admitted Ross Brawn.

The first grand prix of the season was to prove him wrong as Michael won in a canter while Mika Häkkinen retired.

The German went straight to the front and left the Finn behind tenth by tenth until the latter was forced out by a broken suspension on lap 26. With his main adversary out of the way Michael slowed towards the end of the race to rack up his fifth consecutive victory from David Coulthard. *"I reduced the pace at the end as we hadn't done a lot of race distance testing and I wasn't sure how reliable the car was,"* said the world champion later.

The 'Regenmeister' strikes again!

In Malaysia two weeks later the race looked like turning into a walk-over for the two Ferraris just after the start with Michael ahead of Rubens Barrichello. *"At the end of lap 2 I thought that the race was already over,"* admitted Schumacher after the finish.

But this was without taking the weather into account. The sun had been scorching hot since the start of the weekend when a sudden storm, the likes of which can only be found in the tropics, hit the Sepang circuit, sowing indescribable confusion. The Ferraris went off and then there was a mix-up in the pits as they both stopped at the same time with Rubens ahead of Michael. Due to an error the Brazilian's car was missing a rain tyre and Barrichello did not want to rejoin until it was fitted blocking the German who had to wait his turn losing over seventy-two seconds.

Once the race got under way again Michael gave one of his virtuoso displays. Passing on the left or the right lapping five seconds quicker than all the others, overtaking three cars per lap he climbed up from eleventh to first place in just six laps! It was an exhibition of driving that will go down in the annals of motor sport.

It was also difficult for some of his rivals to stomach and after the race an indignant chorus of voices claimed that the Ferraris were using traction control, the only explanation for their speed in the wet. Traction control authorised from the Spanish Grand Prix onwards was forbidden at that moment. Theoretically at least as it was impossible to check whether a car was exploiting it or not.

Rain-soaked Interlagos

Curiously enough at the Brazilian Grand Prix Michael only finished second in the rain. Once David Coulthard got past him all Michael saw was the rear end of the McLaren as he was unable to match its pace which surprised many on-lookers given the German's talent in the wet. He himself refused to advance any explanation after the race and was not in the best of moods. *"I'm not happy but that's normal, isn't it?"* said the world champion. *"The car didn't work as I'd have liked and I couldn't do anything about David today. We didn't really adopt rain settings like the McLarens did: we chose a kind of compromise that didn't work right from the start. I also went off several times which is fairly unusual for me."*

Sad day for the Tifosi

At Imola the atmosphere in the stands was pretty upbeat just before the start. The Ferraris were not that well-placed on the grid with Michael fourth and Rubens sixth. The Italian press filled column inches with the explanations given by the drivers for their relatively poor qualifying performance due to their choice of hard tyres which, they claimed, was the right one for the race.

However, from the start it was obvious that they had gone in the wrong direction. While Ralf Schumacher made a perfect getaway his brother was passed by Jarno Trulli and finished the first lap in fifth place before giving way to Juan Pablo Montoya, Oliver Panis and then his team-mate on lap 4. His car was in trouble: *"I had a problem with my gearbox,"* explained Michael after the race. *"In any case it wasn't my weekend. The race was difficult and it all ended with a problem that we haven't yet identified but which seems linked to the bodywork on the left-hand front wheel."* He retired. *"You can't win all the time,"* he said, *"but it seems that our rivals have managed to make up the advantage we had over them. We still have a lot of work to get done this season."*

A lap too far

A mind-blowing end to the race! A real turn up for the books! When Mika Häkkinen began the last of the sixty-five laps of the Spanish Grand Prix he had a 25 second lead over Michael Schumacher; an eternity on the F1 scale. The Finn's victory looked a foregone conclusion.

But his car had other ideas. In the chicane following the pits straight his MP4-16 suddenly slowed and ground to a smoking halt on the side of the track a few hundred metres further on. It was all over. Thus, a very surprised Schumacher found himself on the top step of the rostrum after battling with an off-form Ferrari for twenty laps. *"Frankly, when I passed Mika's car I really felt sorry for him"*, commented the German driver. *"His second refuelling stop was better than ours, and he drove an error-free race: our duel reminded me of the good old days! It was a real shock to see him stopped a few hundred metres from the finish."*

Tactics in Austria

Seventy-first lap of the race. Jean Todt perched on the pit wall asked Rubens Barrichello, who was about to finish second, to move over and let Michael Schumacher through. The Brazilian had led for thirty-one out of the seventy-one laps of the grand prix but his dreams of victory were turning into a nightmare.

Finally, just a few metres from the line 'Rubinho' slowed and let Michael past. *"I waited for the last corner as it wasn't easy to drive flat-out and concentrate on the orders on the screen while at the same time thinking about what was written in my contract about giving way to Michael. Listening to Jean Todt asking me to let him though on several occasions wasn't easy,"* said Barrichello afterwards.

For Michael on the other hand, things were simple. *"I'm very happy that Rubens let me through,"* he explained, *"because after Mika's retirement it's very clear who Mclaren is going to give preferential treatment to. We have to bear that in mind. Imagine me losing the championship by two points at the end of the season! It'd be absurd. Scoring points through team orders is part of motor racing. F1 includes many things like a lot of pressure, a lot of money. All that matters is winning the championship. McLaren did the same thing in the past. In the next few races you'll see what their decision will be concerning Mika and David."*

Monaco in a canter

"It was a fairly easy race," smiled Michael afterwards admitting that he did not really have to struggle to rack up his fifth win of the year in Monaco. In fact, during the seventy-eight lap race his only battle was maintaining his concentration. *"Somebody asked me why I didn't jump for joy on the rostrum,"* he said. *"Quite frankly I wasn't excited*

enough to do that. It wasn't an exceptional victory. Nothing special happened during this grand prix; at least nothing that warranted an outburst of joy on the rostrum. It's always satisfying to win in Monaco as it's rather special. But this time it wasn't very difficult."

Ralf gets the upper hand

What a duel! After a mind-blowing chase between the Schumacher brothers finally it was Ralf who won the Canadian Grand Prix, his second victory of the season after San Marino.

Michael made the best start and led his younger brother into the first corner. Over the following laps the Ferrari driver tried to shake off the Williams which had no problems matching the pace of the red car. When Michael stopped to refuel Ralf really put the hammer down and made up enough time to enable him to rejoin in the lead after his own stop on lap 51. Victory was his for the taking. *"I tried to really push before Ralf stopped,"* commented Michael, *"but with a heavier fuel load I had no real chance."*

Michael back on the winning trail

Now the pressure was coming from Williams not McLaren. Michael scored another victory in the European Grand Prix on the Nürburgring after fighting off the increasingly competitive Williams-BMWs in the hands of his brother and Colombian Juan Pablo Montoya throughout the race.

Before the race Michael had a big scare. He was out on a reconnaissance lap in his spare car when it stopped on the far side of the circuit. *"It was the worst place possible, the furthest from the pits,"* he related. *"I really wondered how the hell I was going to get back to the pits before they closed. It was a very strange feeling to see my chances suddenly evaporating. Then I saw a scooter but there was no key. And just then someone arrived with the key. I said to myself I'd just about enough time to make it back but I didn't even look at my watch to be sure."*

Battle was joined from the start. Michael had to squeeze his brother towards the pit wall to keep his lead. *"I didn't know what Ralf's strategy was but I knew that we both had to stop twice,"* explained the German after the race. *"Thus, there was no question of letting him get ahead. When I saw him slipping through on the inside I had to use the rules to limit, namely, to change direction once so I tightened the line. I had no other choice."*

In the early stages of the race the younger Schumacher was glued to the leader's tail. *"I was in relative control of the situation. I only had one real scare. When I braked late for the hairpin I left the door slightly open but there*

was no reason for me to make life easy for Ralf. I like racing against him because we always leave each other enough room. It doesn't really matter which of us wins." Once Ralf was out of contention after a harsh penalty for crossing the white line on the pit exit, Michael had to fend off Montoya. Which he did successfully.

Michael's half-century

Michael is usually fairly demonstrative on the rostrum and at Magny-Cours his win seemed to make him even happier than usual. *"That victory really gave me pleasure,"* he stated in the post-race press conference. *"It was really tough but great fun. It's my fiftieth win and that's an important number. My brother and my team-mate were on the rostrum with me and I've increased my lead in the world championship. Everything's roses. It was a crucial race for me."*

His fiftieth win brought him closer to Alain Prost's record of fifty-one. *"I think people often misunderstand me on the importance I give to this kind of record. The number one aim is the world championship title, not statistics. I'm delighted to have fifty victories but that's not the main objective. It does mean something to me but it's secondary."*

Unhappy with six points

Michael was in a really black mood after Silverstone. He had not won the British Grand Prix and in the race he was overtaken by Häkkinen and Juan Pablo Montoya. When he left the rostrum and someone asked him if he had run into trouble or if he had let Mika Häkkinen past as he was no longer a threat the German looked furious. *"Of course! It's obvious, I parked on the side of the track and waved him through!"*

Michael's bad humour was down to his car's performance which did not come up to his expectations. *"I had a completely different car today from yesterday,"* he complained afterwards. *"It was very difficult to drive and we'll have to look into that with the engineers. It was about 100 kilos heavier with the fuel load than in practice but above all it was badly balanced and too slow. "* However, his second place allied to Coulthard's retirement put him into a very strong position for his fourth world championship. *"Of course, these six points are important for the title but I'll keep on fighting until it's settled."*

At Hockenheim two weeks later Michael was victim of a rare mechanical failure on his Ferrari. He was fourth on the grid, started normally and immediately had a gearbox problem which prevented him from changing up. Burti starting from the rear of the grid in his Prost had his line of vision blocked by another car and hit the rear of the Ferrari. *"I saw him coming in my rear view mirror but I had no room to let him through,"* Michael explained. *"It was one hell of an impact but it could've been worse."*

Crowned in Hungary

A week before the race Luca Di Montezemolo, the Ferrari President, asked the team to win the championship in Hungary. He wanted to get it over and done with.

The team arrived in Budapest full of determination with a car modified to suit the Hungaroring. A few minutes before the race a Ferrari mechanic said that tension was running at an all time high in the Ferrari camp. The title was almost within their grasp: they just had to win it!

And that was what Michael Schumacher did. Without problems; He started from pole, went straight into the lead and was never threatened. *"I didn't really think it was going to be this weekend,"* he said after the rostrum ceremony. *"I had a bad feeling and it wasn't until three laps from the end that I began to believe it was over. And that was when I started to get jumpy!"*

Once he had taken the chequered flag (equalling Prost's record 51 wins) he felt emotions that he did not manage to describe but which caused him to burst into tears in the post-race press conference. *"Perhaps I'm not too bad a driver but I'm not much good at expressing my feelings,"* he admitted. It's just marvellous for me and the team. They're fantastic, hard-working, very human, people. They're quite simply the best! "

Compared to the cliff-hanging duels of the previous years the 2001 title seemed to have been rather easy. Michael was, however, very satisfied. *"I don't think this title makes me feel less proud than the others. If you take into account all the opportunities that our rivals missed you realise that they were pretty competitive and we had to fight. With the exception of the first two grands prix they made us work very hard,"* was how he summed it up.

But the season was not over yet as there were still four races left to go. Michael said that his motivation was still intact: *"I'm here to win and I always want to come first,"* he concluded. *"If I screw up at Spa in two weeks, nobody will say to me 'you drove a good race in Budapest. ' I'll be blamed for my mistake. It's these special exigencies that make Formula 1 so unique. In addition, I feel I've got*

enough inner drive to continue to give my all even though the championship is over."

Number 52!

As his main rivals the Williams-BMWs self-destructed at Spa Michael had a fairly easy race. He took the lead on lap 1 and when Fisichella held up the McLarens he only had himself to fight against. Which almost did for him as he went off on lap 17 after losing concentration. *"There are a lot of buttons on the steering wheel and I was playing with them when I went a bit wide but luckily I was able to get the car back."*

With his fifty-second victory he became the outright record holder. *"It's nice beating this score and in addition winning on this circuit is always a bit special. This is where I made my debuts and where I won my first grand prix. We're not too far from home either."*

At Monza a very gloomy atmosphere reigned in the paddock. The attacks of 11th September had happened only a few days before and the Scuderia decided to race without sponsors on the car. Michael , who was complete shattered by what had happened, was in no mood to drive. He finished fourth without really trying. In addition, he did not want to go to the USA saying that he preferred to stay at home. However, a brief phone call from Bernie Ecclestone - who threatened to cancel his points if he did not go to Indianapolis - persuaded him to change his mind.

Finally, the USA Grand Prix weekend went off without problems and Michael came home second behind Mika Häkkinen.

And one for the road!

Right from the start Michael left his rivals in no doubt that he wanted to win the Japanese Grand Prix on the Suzuka circuit the last one of the season. By the end of lap 1 he was 3.6 secs ahead and by lap 2 the gap was over 6 seconds! Mind-boggling. *"Our tyres gave us an advantage when they were new and we knew they wouldn't last,"* explained Schumacher after the race. *"I tried to take advantage of it as we didn't know if the Williams were on a one or two stop strategy."* With this victory the German broke the record for the number of points scored with 801 as opposed to Prost's 798.5. It was total success. *"I 'd say it was a perfect season from all points of view,"* declared Michael. *"It's really special to finish the year with a win, especially after the two difficult races we've just had. It's fantastic for the whole team."*

CHAPTER 10

2002: Raising the game even more

After the Scuderia's astounding success in 2001 it seemed utopian to expect a repeat performance in 2002. Thus, for once Luca Di Montezemolo the Ferrari President did not ask his team to do better than the pervious season! During the 2002 launch he limited himself to saying that he hoped for the same degree of success as in 2001. And yet the team managed to improve on its already brilliant 2001 performance as Michael Schumacher was crowned F1 world champion on the evening of the French Grand Prix after eleven races out of seventeen, an extraordinary achievement. Two grands prix later in Hungary by adding up the totals of both drivers Ferrari won the Constructors' Championship for the twelfth time.

The season, though, had begun with a question mark hanging over Ferrari. The new F1-2002 was not ready and still suffered from a few reliability problems! And so the team preferred to begin the year with the well-tested and very quick 2001 car. During the last grand prix of the 2001 season at Suzuka the team had raced a hybrid version which contained the main elements of the 2002 chassis - and it was extraordinarily quick with Michael Schumacher being two seconds faster than his rivals in the twistier part of the circuit! It certainly seemed that the 2002 car had that little bit extra mainly in high-speed corners.

A test team for the tyres

As McLaren had opted for Michelin for the 2002 season the French manufacturer was obliged to divide its efforts between two top teams, Williams and McLaren. On the other hand Bridgestone was able to devote all its energy to Ferrari; thus to the world championship title with Schumacher. In this way the Scuderia had total support from the Japanese manufacturer enabling it to set up a test team whose only task was Bridgestone tyre testing. To this end Ferrari hired Luciano Burti the former Prost driver noted for his miraculous escape from his huge accident in the 2001 Belgian Grand Prix.

This test squad enabled the Japanese company to understand perfectly how the Italian cars worked. The win in the first race of the season in Melbourne showed just how well the system gelled between Ferrari and Bridgestone. After the race Michael had nothing but praise for the quality of the Japanese tyres. *"As soon as the tyres were up to temperature, I was able to pull away easily,"* he confirmed. *"Bridgestone gave us a really great product."* The bespoke tyres provided an added advantage to those enjoyed by the Scuderia, namely, its driver's skills and extraordinary chassis.

An eventful start

Michael was on pole with Montoya beside him on the front row, a situation that promised an explosive start to the second race in Malaysia. And it was as the Colombian was quicker off the line than the German and had to pull to the outside of the track as Michael dived for the inside. Both men arrived side by side in the first corner. If Juan Pablo kept his line he would be on the right trajectory for the following hairpin and would take the lead. Then the Ferrari and the Williams hit each other breaking the red car's nose and slowing the Colombian. Michael was forced to pit to have the nose changed and Montoya fell back finishing lap 1 in eleventh place. For both it was the start of a fantastic comeback that was the highlight of the grand prix.

The Williams driver got up to sixth when he was penalised by the Stewards for having caused an avoidable collision. *"I'm furious about this penalty,"* grumbled the Colombian after the race. *"I was on the outside of the corner and I left enough room for Michael to pass but his car understeered and hit me. That's all there is to say. For sure I didn't leave him a lot of room as I didn't want to end up on the dirty part of the track but he could've got by. I didn't expect him to brake. He's a racing driver and I don't think he hit me on purpose. It was a race incident, that's all and I don't see why I should have been penalised."*

Obviously Michael did not share the Colombian's point of view: *"he squeezed me and I really didn't have enough room to pass."* Concerning the penalty the German agreed with his rival. *"This penalty wasn't justified. We've seen much worse that was not sanctioned. I feel that this type of decision is not taken in a coherent way. It has to be changed."*

The collision between the two hard men of the paddock was just another incident to be added to their file. The tension between the two drivers separated by only two points was not about to fall.

Number two at Interlagos

They did it again at Interlagos. This time the starting order was reversed with Juan Pablo on pole and Michael in second place. It looked like fireworks in the first corner but the action came a little further on. The Williams made a worse start than the Ferrari and tried to squeeze it in the left-right after the start. Juan Pablo braked too late and veered to the outside. *"I braked at the very limit at the end of the straight but Juan Pablo hit the brakes even later. It was clear to me that he was going to miss the corner,"* said Michael after the grand prix.

The Colombian came back on his line and found himself side-by-side with the German who was now on the inside. Having lost out on the corner the Williams tried to get alongside the Ferrari on the following straight. Montoya then hit the rear of the Italian car and lost his front wing and with it his chances of victory. *"I have to say that Juan Pablo was very fair-play as he left me enough room to pass,"* declared Michael. *"When he hit me I didn't feel anything; I don't know what he did. My car wasn't damaged."*

All Michael had to do now was to control his lead over Ralf Schumacher. Rubens Barrichello hit the front briefly but he was on a two-stop strategy and was not a threat for the German. He broke down shortly afterwards.

Towards the end of the race after refuelling Ralf began to pull in the Ferrari tenth by tenth but the younger brother could not overtake the elder one. *"I knew that Ralf had only one spot where he could pass me, in the first corner,"* analysed Michael. *"All I had to do was to take the right line out of the previous corner and make sure I had a big enough lead on the straight. In the slow section I didn't really push; I tried to drive without making a blunder as it's impossible to pass there."*

Michael's second win of the season gave him an eight point lead over his brother. Montoya after a race against the clock finished fifth putting him ten points behind his sworn enemy.

Thanks to Bridgestone

Michael won the fourth grand prix of the year at Imola in a canter. He went into the lead from the start which he lost momentarily during refuelling. His sixty-two laps of the circuit was a doddle. *"I'm very happy with this victory,"* he commented after leaving the rostrum. *"Last year we failed here and this time we've managed to make up for it in front of the Tifosi. It's been a very special grand prix for me."*

So what was the secret of his domination? For him it was due mainly to a new type of tyre provided by Bridgestone. *"I didn't think I'd have a such an advantage today,"* he continued. *"Qualifying showed that our rivals were very close and I was expecting a tough battle. Bridgestone has produced a tyre that is much more constant than usual. Although this win is down to the car as a whole, it is due essentially to the quality of the new tyres."*

For Rubens Barrichello his second place enabled to score his first points of the year. It was the first of several doubles. In this race - not for the last time during the season - Ferrari found itself without serious rivals.

Finally, Nick Heidfeld stopped four times and finished tenth behind Felippe Massa. It's called 'getting your knickers in a twist!'

Schumi's walkover

The number 1 Ferrari had just crossed the finishing line and the loud speakers in the press room were hooked up to the Scuderia's internal radio system. Ross Brawn, the technical director congratulated his driver: *"Bravo Michael. What a great race."*

"It's you who should be congratulated for giving me such a fantastic car. It's a sheer pleasure to drive," replied the German on his lap of honour as he waved to the crowds.

Michael led the Spanish Grand Prix from start to finish and was never threatened.

Once again it was his team-mate who was hit by gremlins. Due to a gearbox problem Rubens couldn't even cover the formation lap.

Austria: a hotly contested decision

The Austrian Grand Prix on the Spielberg circuit caused a public outcry. A torrent of whistles and boos greeted Barrichello and Schumacher when they came into the press room for the traditional post-race conference. It was a never-before-seen welcome in the memories of any journalist.

The German, who was second for most of the race, won the Austrian Grand Prix after Rubens Barrichello, following team orders, moved over to let him through in the final metres.

Michael asked his team-mate to step up onto the highest step of the rostrum in his place to render homage to him. It was a big mistake from a protocol point of view. The FIA used it as a pretext to sanction the German and his team which was fined a million dollars a few weeks later.

The press conference was anything but pleasant for Michael Schumacher who was subjected to some very tough questioning on his day's win. *"It's obvious I don't like what's happened here,"* admitted the world champion. *"I get no pleasure out of this victory seeing as how the season is unfolding. Last year we had exactly the same situation but the championship was much closer. I didn't think it was necessary today. This morning I was asked if there would be any team tactics and I answered that I didn't think so. And then suddenly over the radio I was told that Rubens was going to let me past. It was a team decision and it came from Ferrari, from Messrs Di Montezemolo and Todt. You must remember that our sponsors spend fortunes with a single aim, winning the world title. This has to be done as soon as possible as you never know what can happen. If we just missed out the championship, imagine how ridiculous we'd look!"*

The German thanked his team-mate for his 'gift.' *"Rubens drove a great race. He was quicker than me throughout the weekend and his gesture shows how much we believe in each other. I'd like to thank him for the points but I get no pleasure out of the win."*

Questioned about the credibility of his future title Michael had to defend himself tooth and nail. *"Such tactics are part and parcel of motor racing. It's often been seen in the past. Williams, McLaren and Sauber have all done it. Some people understand, others don't. Overall I'm in favour of team tactics but not what happened today. I couldn't do anything. After being told I even thought about disobeying orders and slowing down to let Rubens win. When he slowed, I slowed too but he braked and I went past without even having the time to think about it. It all happened very quickly. Now we're sitting quietly and we've got the time to reflect. Not like when I was in the car. If I could I'd roll back time and reverse the result. It's too late now; We have to turn the page."*

Many people were already criticising Ferrari for its outrageous domination of the championship and the team orders controversy only added fuel to the flames. While the Scuderia did not need such tactics, these have existed since the beginning of motor racing and have never been the subject of much discussion.

En fanfare

At Monaco Michael came home second behind David Coulthard who led from start to finish. The German's six points was a good damage limiting exercise. Another win in Canada showed that Dame Fortune was on his side as he had an engine go during the warm up, the final half-hour's practice before the race itself. If his V10 had lasted an additional four laps it would have blown up during the grand prix. He scored another victory and his most dangerous rival, Juan Pablo Montoya, ground to a smoking halt due to a damaged engine.

A second place in the European Grand Prix behind Rubens Barrichello (no team orders this time!) was the prelude to a remarkable series of wins in England, France, Germany and Belgium (as this book is going to press). This enabled Michael to rack up his fifth F1 World Championship title in France and in Belgium he set a new record for the number of wins in a season (ten so far).

Thanks to his fifth title Michael has equalled the record set in 1957 by Juan Manual Fangio. *"I was very relaxed all through the weekend,"* he said after his fantastic French Grand Prix success. *"Frankly I didn't even think about the title as I didn't feel it was going to happen here. When I saw Rubens retire and I realised just how much quicker I was than Juan Pablo, I said to myself, 'well maybe there's a chance.' Then after my penalty Kimi Räikkönen was going so fast that I didn't believe in it at all. And when I passed him the whole weight of the championship thudded down on my shoulders. It was very tough, the hardest five laps of my career."*

Once he had done the job he could give full vent to his joy. *"I was very moved and I admit that I shed a few tears in my helmet. It's my fifth title and each one is special in its own way. You never get used to that type of feeling."*

135

Captions

2001: Austrian Grand Prix. A pensive Michael Schumacher finished in second place after his team asked Rubens Barrichello to let him past
Photo: Thierry Gromik

2001: Monaco Grand Prix fourth victory of the season for Michael Schumacher
Photo: Thierry Gromik

2001: Brazilian Grand Prix. After two wins of the trot in Australia and Malaysia Michael finished second in the rain behind David Coulthard. His settings were ill-adapted to the wet track
Photo: Thierry Gromik

2001: Belgian Grand Prix. Schumacher's eighth win of the season. After a first lap battle he waltzed away from the rest of the field on his favourite circuit
Photo: Thierry Gromik

2001: Hungarian Grand Prix. Michael Schumacher scored his second consecutive title in his Ferrari. Not since Nigel Mansell in 1992 had a driver won the world championship so early in the season
Photo: Thierry Gromik

2002: Brazilian Grand Prix. Michael started from the front row and ran up his second win of the year after that of Melbourne
Photo: Thierry Gromik

2002: German Grand Prix. This was the first time that Michael won at Hockenheim in a Ferrari after setting his first pole position on the German circuit
Photo: Thierry Gromik

2002: French Grand Prix. Luca Di Montezemolo, the Ferrari President, joined the whole team to celebrate Michael Schumacher's third consecutive world title
Photos: LAT

In a world of his own

Five world championships do not come about by accident. Winning a third with Ferrari was the fruit of unwavering commitment.

As we have seen in the previous chapters Michael Schumacher had an unprecedented rise to fame in motor racing meeting the right people - Jürgen Dilk, Willy Weber and the people from Mercedes-Benz - at the right moment. But as other drivers have found out having all the right elements in place does not always lead to success. One has to have the talent to make one's mark immediately as without this it is impossible to reach the top rung of the ladder.

The best of them all?

Michael's results throughout his career and especially in Formula 1 speak for themselves. The majority of experts in F1 be they team managers, journalists and engineers all say that Michael Schumacher, the best driver of his generation, has moved up a step in the hierarchy of all-time greats to join men like Juan Manual Fangio, Alain Prost and Ayrton Senna

In relation to these three or four or even five-times world champions Michael had already achieved the exploit of becoming the youngest ever double F1 world champion in the history of the sport. He won his fifth title at the age of 33 which leaves him ample time to beat the record he shares with Fangio. During the summer of 2002 Willy Weber, his manager, stated that his driver would go on racing into his forties. It is a subject on which Michael refuses to be drawn and just says that he will continue for a long time - as long as he gets pleasure out of driving - without setting any deadline.

Even though he has equalled Fangio's record of five F1 world titles he refuses to compare himself with the famous Argentinean whom he admires as being the greatest.

Comparing the fifties to the present day is impossible. When Fangio raced people wore small helmets and goggles, had no seat belts and no protection in case of accidents. They drove very powerful cars with narrow tyres which slid all over the place. In films from that era we can see drivers who had to master slides and literally manhandle their cars around corners in a way that seems almost unbelievable today.

Aerodynamic grip has eliminated all that and the cars look as if they are on rails and when one slides it is usually because the driver is pushing too hard or has made a mistake.

It is for all these reasons that Michael declines comparison with Juan-Manual Fangio in spite of having the same number of titles as well as being in a position to beat the record in the years to come.

He declares that he has a lot of admiration for the driver he considers the best. *"I'm in complete awe of the drivers of the era,"* he explains. *"The way they drove has nothing in common with us and that's why we can't compare ourselves with them. Even if we have the same number of titles my talent doesn't measure up to Fangio's!"*

He acknowledged that he had been born with natural talent which might possibly have remained latent had he not worked hard at developing it from the age of four. And had he not also shown such intelligence in his motor racing apprenticeship. As Jochen Mass - the German driver who was his guide in the Mercedes-Benz Junior team - stated, Michael was always willing to listen to advice. He paid close attention to all the details that could help him progress and knew how to learn from his mistakes. Thus he never made the same one twice.

These qualities alone would not have been enough to make Michael the exceptional driver that he has become. Several aspiring youngsters have had the same capacities. What distinguishes the German from them is his extraordinary facility to adapt to all kinds of new situations be it a new circuit, a new car or both at the same time. He has shown this on numerous occasions in his career: for example when he went from one formula to another or each time he raced on a new circuit. "*What surprised me the most about Michael was that almost as soon as he got into the car he was quick straight off,*" explained Peter Sauber. "*He did not take long to adapt and lapped quickly right away. As time went by his team-mates reduced the gap and after thirty or forty laps the differences were minimal. Each time, however, Michael set very quick times in his early laps . He has a natural ability to find the limits of a car immediately. This, I think, is what sets him apart from all the other drivers.*"

An awesome capacity to adapt which Andrea De Cesaris and Nelson Piquet never got over (see chapter 2). This faculty is not the only one that makes the kid from Kerpen stand out from other drivers. If this almost instantaneous ability to get a feel for a car is already an enormous advantage it alone does not explain his speed. While this is impossible to calculate exactly except when driving the very same car many observers reckon that Michael Schumacher is at least half-a-second quicker than his rivals.

A second worth millions

It was this latter quality which Ferrari bet on when it signed the German in the summer of 1995. And it was also why the Scuderia decided to invest the 25 - and from 1997 - 30 million dollars which Schumacher demanded as salary. The team's budget is obviously secret but must be in the region of 150 to 200 million dollars annually.

For the engineers gaining half-a-second a lap represents months of work, hundreds of hours in the wind tunnel plus heavy investment in research in all areas including the engine, suspension and aerodynamics. Thus, it made sense for a team as powerful as Ferrari to invest 30 million dollars in a driver knowing that it will achieve the same result.

For his fellows drivers the question remains as to how Michael Schumacher manages to be quicker than his team-mates. It is common knowledge as some teams have pointed out in public that his team-mates have had to play second fiddle. This was the case for several drivers in the past like Johnny Herbert and Eddie Irvine both of whom had a reputation as hot shoes before coming up against Michael.

Herbert has often spoken about how Michael manoeuvred to prevent him from making his mark. "*The first time I got into the car during the 1994-95 winter I was faster than Michael straight away,*" said the British driver. "*And funnily enough as soon as the season began I didn't do any more private testing. I arrived at the grands prix on the Thursday with no pre-defined set up and I had to spend all of Friday trying to balance the car. In the meantime, Michael got on with the job calmly preparing for Saturday's qualifying and the race. He had already done private testing before each event on similar type circuits according to the grand prix to come. On Friday morning his setup was already fine tuned and it was impossible to equal his times. I wasn't fighting with the same weapons as him...*"

This testimony and the obvious unequal treatment of which his team-mates have been the victims seem to suggest that it is impossible to compare their talent to his. Thus, the famous half-second which Michael contributes is not worth all that much when weighed against his talent to manoeuvre his team politically in order to diminish the role of any uppity team-mate.

This is a theory frequently put forward by his detractors but one that can easily be refuted by the German's first two grands prix.

At Spa in 1991 it would seem difficult to accuse the Jordan team of privileging a debutante driver over its star of the era, Andrea De Cesaris. At Monza for the following race it would be even more ridiculous to suspect the Benetton squad of favouring Michael over three-times world champion, Nelson Piquet - although in this case political considerations could have pushed Benetton to show the Brazilian that his talent was not equal to his reputation.

Nonetheless on both circuits Schumacher dominated team-mates who were both much more experienced than him.

Thus his speed cannot be attributed solely to his ability to influence his team. Of course it is true that over the years he has always managed to orient the development of the cars in the direction that suits him best.

That is why in 1994 when he was absent for two grands prix after being suspended by the FIA, the two Benettons were completely off the pace and ended up in the middle of the grid while in the hands of Michael the car was often on pole.

During these two events it is difficult to accuse the team of a favouring a driver who was at home in his Monaco apartment! In fact even with all the efforts of the team concentrated on thém the two Benetton drivers at Monza and Estoril - the races in question - were unable to exploit the car as Michael Schumacher would have done. This was not only because of lesser talent but also because the B194 was literally tailor-made for the German and was very difficult for anyone else to drive who had a different style.

To explain his superiority and his extra half-second's speed one has to study his driving style. This is where his secret lies. It is obviously jealously protected but it has been pierced over the years by an in-depth analysis of his performances.

Johnny Herbert gives the reader an initial glimpse. *"I don't much like comparing myself to Michael Schumacher,"* he said. *"For sure he's a bit quicker than me but the difference wasn't enormous in 1995. It was essentially a question of self-confidence. Michael had been with Benetton for four years and knew everybody in the team. He knew the car inside out and was very sure of himself. In fact, if the gap between us didn't demoralise me too much it's because I knew the inside story. Michael has a very particular style of driving. He has this thing I've never met with any other driver which gives him an advantage that I was unable to overcome. And I was already too old at the time to try and modify my style and adopt it to his. The difference was too great."*

Seen from the side of the track or in front of a TV screen it is difficult to pick out the styles of drivers except in particular circumstances. From one car to another it is easier to recognise Michael Schumacher's talent. *"When he was on the limit the back end of his car was dancing around this limit. The other drivers seemed to be on rails. It was not at all the same thing,"* commented Julian Bailey who raced in Macao in 1989 the same time as the German.

The truth that dare not speak its name!

Other drivers, though, have great difficulty in admitting Schumacher's superiority. Which would be an act of implicit self-denigration! *"I don't think that Michael is in any way special in relation to the others,"* states David Coulthard. *"Of course he's quick, very quick though I can't really explain why. Maybe its quite simply because his chassis is better balanced."*

Heinz-Harald Frentzen who knows Michael's style very well as he drove with him at Mercedes-Benz when both were racing in the Endurance Championship shares the same sceptical viewpoint. *"It's impossible to know whether Michael has a secret or not. Nevertheless each driver has a style even if the differences are tiny. For sure, he has immense talent but all I can say is that his driving is a skilful mixture of aggressiveness and flow."*

In driving schools people admit that Schumacher has opted for a very particular style. *"It's very possible that he has developed a new type of driving,"* says Serge Saulnier, the manager of the Promotec F3 team and former driving instructor at the Winfield School at Magny-Cours where the majority of French F1 drivers learned their trade. *"Alain Prost launched the fashion of heavy barking in tight corners which enabled him to fit harder springs thus improving the overall handling of the car. Since then everybody has copied him."* In 1995, Olivier Panis was able to compare his telemetry data with that of Schumacher who did a few laps in the Ligier. He saw that the German had a very strange way of playing with the accelerator. Instead of blipping it he used the pedal in a very fluid way. *"In reality he did everything possible to maintain constant speed in corners so as not to upset the car's ride height."*

The present day F1s are so finely tuned aerodynamically that the slightest variation in the ride height reduces performance. Schumacher's method is a solution for optimising balance in the corners. *"I'd guess that he's spent many hours with his engineers refining his style to get as close as possible to computer simulations,"* continues Saulnier. *"He's not the only one to have understood what has to be done but he's obviously the one who's got it right. That's what singles out the great champions."*

A special technique

Finally under questioning Michael Schumacher spoke about his cornering technique. *"You have to feel the car, feel it with your whole body which sends this information to the brain and this in turn transmits it into the movements of the steering wheel. That, I think, is what makes part of the difference between drivers. Some manage to get a feel for their chassis but are unable to transmit this to the steering wheel. In my opinion, the secret of speed consists of taking corners on the limit while balancing the car with the accelerator to keep it stable. The majority of drivers try to do it but some are too jerky which costs them time. I really do my best to be gentle with the accelerator to the very edge and above all to stay that way all through the corner. Other drivers find their car's limit on the exit but they're not there on the entry or in the middle; it's all very well to be on the limit on the exit of a cor-*

ner but it's impossible to make up for the time lost on the entry. Over a whole lap that's maybe what makes the difference for pole. And over a race it's what perhaps make the difference between victory and second or third place."

Braking after everybody else

His braking technique is very special. From the trackside it is mind-blowing to see how late he brakes in certain corners in relation to his rivals. This is how he explains it: *"For me braking points are made by the brake marks left by the other drivers. You can see the places where the flat bottoms have touched the tarmac under heavy braking. My aim is always to brake after the last of these marks. In general I also have reference points on the side of the track but at the last moment I look at the track itself and the corner which tunes me in to the final braking point."*

To the German his talent is natural. *"I don't want to label myself the best F1 driver,"* he explains. *"But obviously I'm very happy when I'm told that I am. In F1, people always try to make you out as extraordinary. Of course, I can drive quickly but when I'm alone I think about myself and I say that one needs a whole lot more than being able to drive quickly to become an extraordinary person!"*

However, one of the most extraordinary faces of Michael's talent is his ability to be driving on the edge without it occupying him 100%! All drivers talk to their pit by radio and generally the exchange is limited to the basic minimum: an impending pit stop, confirmation of an order etc... Limited exchanges which only take place on the straight when the driver can relax momentarily.

Schumacher has time to spare. The Benetton team still remember his habit of joking on the radio or talking about this and that. Some days he even began singing while driving! This insight shows to what extent he is master of his situation. *"Michael talks a lot on the radio,"* confirmed Bernard Dudot, the Renault Sport chief engineer who worked with the German during the 1995 season. *"He wants to know where his rivals are; what their refuelling strategy is. He absorbs everything and decides his own tactics as a result. And all this time he's driving flat out!"*

Pat Symonds his race engineer at Benetton at the time remembers Michael joking on the radio making comments on his rivals that had his engineers on the pit wall doubled up with laughter!

The German says that his ability to remain detached comes from the leeway that he still has under his right foot: *"I make the distinction between driving flat out and driving at*

100%", he explained to the magazine F1 Racing. *"100% means driving as quickly as possible while keeping an eye on fuel consumption and the state of your tyres. This means that it's not possible to go as fast as the car is capable of going. You have to do a kind of mathematical calculation taking everything into account and go as quickly as possible according to the result. In some grands prix I slowed right down towards the end as it was no longer necessary to push myself to the maximum."*

A heart of oak

This ability to stand back in relation to his driving is also illustrated by his astonishing calm. Numerous medical tests have shown that drivers are sportsmen who put a lot of strain on their hearts. At the start of a grand prix their heartbeat goes up to 220 beats per minute and this rate is maintained during the race at over 180 beats per minute with highs of 190-200 while overtaking.

This is not his case. Thanks to his amazing physical form due to his four to six hours per day exercising and his natural calm, for him a grand prix is the same as a game of chess. Or almost! *"Obviously there are moments when I feel some tension,"* he explains, *"especially on the starting grid. But as soon as the formation lap begins I feel completely calm and I think of nothing except what has to be done in the next few minutes. Sometimes when we come back to the starting grid and we're waiting for the last cars to take up position, I manage to hear my heart beating in spite of the surrounding noise. I see the red lights going off one after another without any particular apprehension. Once you've done a few starts, you know you can do it and you begin to get used to it."*

On the other hand many drivers never get used to the start and feel that their guts are twisted in knots in the minutes before the race at the end of which they are totally exhausted. This is not the case with Michael. He has never collapsed on the rostrum like Nelson Piquet or Nigel Mansell. He has never had to stay in his car for several minutes before being able to get out as was the case for Ayrton Senna. After the 1999 Malaysian Grand Prix run in record heat and humidity he was as cool as a cucumber on the rostrum while Mika Häkkinen looked on the point of passing out.

He explains this difference by his exceptional physical form - far and away the best of the drivers - indeed some like Jacques Villeneuve refuse to train in a gym. *"It's very important to be in top physical form,"* states Schumacher. *"If you're not then you may feel* muscular pain which reduces your ability to drive. Fitness helps one to remain calm and concentrated. If I can keep my heartbeat at 140 beats per minute rather than the 180 of the other drivers I have a big advantage. I do the same job as the other but he's on the edge and I'm not. Sometimes I do feel tired at the end of a race but I recuperate very quickly. All I can say is that if I'm tired then the others must be on the point of fainting! That's why I train four to six hours per day although sometimes I feel really alone in my gym."

The extra-terrestrial

After Michael Schumacher won the 1995 French Grand Prix in his Benetton from Damon Hill's Williams the two drivers turned up for the press conference in very different states. While Hill was dripping with sweat and took a lot of effort to arrange his hair Michael was in top form. Hill slipped his hand through the opening in Schumacher's driving suit and exclaimed: "Not a drop of sweat. This guy's an extra-terrestrial!" Yet another proof of the extra physical capacity which the German has on call during a race before reaching his edge.

Balbir Singh: secrets of a Hindu!

In the paddock few people can make out Balbir Singh. Even drivers have the odd moment to spare but the Hindu physiotherapist is always on the go and has no time to indulge in the latest F1 gossip. Which does not interest him anyway. F1 for him is Michael Schumacher for whom he fills the role of masseur, dietician and physiotherapist.

While today all teams have a physical coach, Balbir Singh uses exotic methods that seem to suit Schumacher down to the ground. "I leant my job in India," he explains, "since then I've redone my exams in Germany but my methods are different from those of European physiotherapists. I've kept a few eastern secrets but don't think you'll get them out of me!"

At the circuit Balbir's day begins in the morning before practice. "Generally, we do a little massage and a little relaxation before Michael gets behind the wheel. Not very long; around twenty-five minutes to get his muscles working and his energy flowing. After practice we don't have much time. Michael is very much in demand; his engineers want him as do the press; his sponsors etc..In the hotel in the evenings we've got much more time and we have a long massage session every day. An hour and a half, sometimes more." No other driver has such iron discipline. "In my opinion Michael is far and away the best prepared of all the drivers," confirms Balbir. "He's in top form as in addition to the massage, he works out in in the gym between four and six hours daily. He doesn't need my advice for that. He's very strong mentally and he does his training programme whatever the weather conditions. It doesn't matter if it's raining or snowing!"

Thanks to Uncle

Balbir Singh was born in India. After being trained as a physiotherapist he left his country to come and work in Germany where he got married. He was living a peaceful life near Bonn.

"I was working in a practice in Koblenz hospital," he recalls. "Michael's uncle was one of my patients and over the years we became friends. One day he left me a message to call him saying that he had some work for me. He told me that Michael was looking for a trainer and was testing several people. I was given an air ticket for Marseilles where I was picked up. It was in November 1995 and he had just started with Ferrari and was doing some private testing at Castellet. I really knew very little about motor sport but I used what I though were the most appropriate massages. I stayed for three days and a few weeks later Michael told me that he would take me on. It was a great day. I couldn't believe it!"

Following Michael 300 days of the year!

Looking after the Ferrari driver is not exactly the easiest of lives. In addition to all the grand prix weekends Michael does a lot of private testing on the Ferrari track at Fiorano plus Monza, Barcelona and elsewhere. Balbir has to follow him to look after his diet and body. For him it is like night and day compared to his well-organised life in Koblenz hospital. "Of course, I'm away from the house some 300 days a year. When I think of my two little boys, it's hard as I miss my family. But it's like that for everybody in F1. I'm philosophical and say to myself that life's not easy."

Whenever you see Michael you can be sure that Balbir Singh is not far away. At the hotel he looks after everything for his driver from his car keys to his racing gloves. At the circuit with a drinks bottle in his hand he scurries back and forth between the pits and the motorhome to make sure that the five-times world champion lacks nothing..

Over time the relationship between the two men had become one of total complicity. "I often go to Michael's house in Vufflens-le-Château to look after his fitness between grands prix," confides Balbir. "I feel completely at home there. His wife Corinna is really charming and I'm treated like a true friend. Michael and I understand each other very well. It's as if we've known each other for a long time and never does he make me feel that he's the boss."

Before being taken on by Schumacher Balbir knew nothing about motor sport. "I didn't even know that Formula 1 existed. It was a world that held no interest for me whatsoever", he recalls today with a smile. *"Bit by bit I'm starting to ask questions about the other cars and drivers. It's all coming together."*

Obviously, he lives F1 through his driver. *"When I have the time, when the food is ready, I watch practice or the race on the monitors in the Ferrari motorhome. Of course I follow Michael almost exclusively and I find that really exciting. Today I'm completely hooked. I can't stay still during a grand prix!"* Proof that Bernie Ecclestone's circus can really get the adrenaline going in a Hindu!

Finally, in addition to the various skills that have been mentioned Michael has a fantastic capacity for understanding technical problems. Like an engineer he is able to spend hours analysing the telemetry data and studying how to improve his car's behaviour. *"Every day I enjoy learning more about technology as it helps to understand a whole raft of reactions of the car. And I love anything that helps me to go quicker."*

He is a real workaholic and is always among the last drivers to leave the paddock. He is ever willing to do private testing and always asks to do the work himself rather than leaving it up to the test driver. *"I get a real kick out of it when the engineers manage to make the car go quicker thanks to the precision of my indications. I could tell them 'do this or do that' on the car and go off and have a coffee or joke with other people but that's not in my nature. I love professional in-depth collaboration with the team. I think that this goes back to my time with Mercedes. I thought then that we weren't working enough and that we could have done more. I was always asking for information."*

Yet again such a capacity for work, such passion for technology which many drivers find boring ranks Michael Schumacher among the greatest. All the great champion racing drivers, without exception, are gifted with this taste for the technical side. Over the past several years Alain Prost and Ayrton Senna were noted for their habit of breaking down the smallest telemetry diagrams and their thirst to know the most arcane details of their cars. They too spent evenings at the track working with their engineers to find solutions that could gain them that extra tenth of a second.

To sum up: Michael Schumacher's talent is a perfect combination of all the qualities found in the great champions. The German rounds off his driving technique and his innate ability to adapt himself to new conditions by his energy, work and an uncanny technical sense.

Perfection does not exist on the earthly plane and those who approach it are often decried by their contemporaries. Michael was very quickly branded with a reputation for being cold, a computer without a soul, and the controversy that tarnished the 1994 season did nothing to improve his image. In 1995, while Germany deified their new hero the rest of the world found him somewhat stand-offish.

There is no doubt that he does not deserve this image generated in many respects by various jealousies. The man that is hidden behind the driver is really the opposite of the pretentious and self-sufficient human being he has too often been labelled. His success has not gone to his head although his renown has obliged him to take certain precautions to protect his privacy.

While the driver in Michael Schumacher is close to perfection the man himself knows how to keep his distance in relation to motor racing. The huge fortune which he has earned has not damaged his sense of values (see chapter 13). This too is part of Michael Schumacher's style.

150

Captions

Michael Schumacher with his motor bike in front of the Monaco port. Since then he has moved to Switzerland
Photo: LAT

Michael is the driver who looks after his physical preparation the best. He spends between four and six hours per day in gyms
Photo: LAT

On the left: Willy Weber, Michael's manager since 1988
On the right: Sabine Kehm, Michael's personal press attaché since the 2000 season
Photos: Steve Domenjoz et LAT

Michael and Corinna in front of their magnificent home in Vufflens-le-Château near Lausanne in Switzerland
Photo: LAT

A relaxed moment in the life of a world champion: Michael and Corinna set off for a bike ride in the surrounding countryside. The five-times world champion loves cycling
Photo: LAT

Michael with his two children Gina Maria and Mick Junior who already drives a kart. And when he doesn't go quickly enough dad gives him a push!
Photo: LAT

The Schumachers love dogs several of which are seen here in the garden of their house in Vufflens-le-Château.
Photos: LAT

"Boo!" Michael knows how not to take himself too seriously contrary to his reputation. Melbourne 1996
Photo: Thierry Gromik

CHAPTER 12

The Schumacher System

Michael Schumacher is exceptional in many respects and not just on the track. He is the highest-paid driver in the history of motor racing and third in the hit parade of the best-paid sportsmen in the world behind two Americans, a basketball player and a boxer.

In 2002 Michael Schumacher's salary at Ferrari was 35 million dollars. In 1996 it was 25 million which was increased to 30 million for 1997, 1998, 1999 and 2000. In addition there are his personal sponsors: 6 million dollars from Nike, 5 from Dekra which in 1999 was replaced by an investment bank, 'Deutsche Vermögensberatung', whose cap Michael must wear at all times in public places except on the rostrum where it is replaced by the tyre manufacturer's. Over the years he has attracted other sponsors such as L'Oréal, the cosmetics giant which appears on the arms of his driving suit and the German jam brand 'Zentis' which pays him 5 million dollars to use his name.

All he had to do for Zentis was to make a short advertising film in which he admires superb plums and then tastes jam made from them. As this film had to be made during the winter Michael was sent to South Africa for a couple of days as it was the only place where an orchard full of plum trees could be found in January!

L'Oréal paid him 6 million dollars to do an advertising film which consisted of a few days' shooting at Ferrari in Maranello. To do a really top job the French company brought in two Hollywood directors who came up with a scenario which showed the Ferrari in the factory wind tunnel which was going at full blast! The fans were then stopped and the driver got out of his car, took off his helmet and rain his hands through his hair which had been blown backwards by the air stream. Michael did the shoot but then telephoned his manager, Willy Weber, to tell him about the film. *"If we let it be shown as it is, we'll look ridiculous,"* he commented. Drivers, of course, never sit in the models being tested in the wind tunnel. In addition, with a helmet protecting his head it is stretching the imagination to believe that his hair would have been blown backwards!

So Willy managed to modify the editing of the film but as the contract signed with L'Oréal made provision for only three days' shooting there was no question of the driver going back to Maranello to make another film. The cosmetics company had to make do with the footage at its disposal to reshoot a more conventional advertising film.

As he has more than enough money to last him a lifetime why does he always accept new advertising contracts - even though in 1999 he said 'that's enough.' *"You must remember that Michael comes from a humble background. When he was young he only had a few Deutschmarks in his pocket so when someone offers him 5 million dollars he would find it indecent to refuse even though he knows full well that he doesn't need the cash."*

From glasses to perfume

In addition to these sums Michael derives income from 'The Michael Schumacher Collection', an original idea from the fertile brain of Willy Weber. The collection consists of all kinds of objects from sunglasses to pens bearing Michael Schumacher's name.

In Germany in 1996 there were already over 220 articles stamped with his name whose prices varied from 5 to 2000 Deutschmarks. It was a huge success and supply was hard put to meet the demand. Since then all kinds of products have been added to the list including pasta, butter, beach sandals and perfume.

To have a product included in the collection the brands contact Willy Weber who gives his agreement against a percentage varying from 10 to 15% per article sold. The collection which is looked after by a Stuttgart-based company, PPM, will have an estimated turn-over of 200 million Deutschmarks (over 102 million Euros). Willy Weber, the driver's manager and project leader, estimates Michael Schumacher's income from that as around 11.5 million Euros.

The idea for the 'Michael Schumacher Collection' came from the driver himself. *"I was always tempted by the project. Ayrton was the only other driver who saw the potential of his own marketing range and developed the concept. I thought I had to do it as I hate the idea of other people making money out of me when we have no relationship. So we decided to get the project up and running and Willy has done a great job. Initial investment was high but we're now on the right track."*

Golden headgear

Another highly profitable source of income, which is not part of the Michael Schumacher Collection, is the red cap with the driver's name on it. Willy Weber using his business cunning has its design changed every year adding a golden edge or modifying its shape or removing the number of the car. This forces the real fans to buy a new cap every year to keep up with the trend.

Each cap is sold for around 40 Deutschmarks and brings in 11 Deutschmarks net profit for the duo. In 1999, no fewer than 2 million caps were sold generating income of 22 million Deutschmarks (11,4 million Euros) from this business alone.

His own magazine

The very active Michael Schumacher's Supporters Club gave Webber the idea of launching a magazine entirely dedicated to the driver. Called the 'Michael Schumacher Magazine' it is published by a company called Pole Position specially created for this purpose. It is a quarterly sold both on news-stands in Germany and through the club which had almost 30 000 members in 2000.

Michael Schumacher relied completely on Willy Webber (see photo page 159, left) to look after requests for media interviews and diverse propositions. In 1995, he was overwhelmed by requests for interviews and took on Heiner Buchinger. Then at the start of the 2000 season he was joined by Sabine Kemm (right-hand photo on page 159). She is a former journalist from the dailies 'Die Welt' and 'Die Süddeutsche' and knows her way round motor sport. It is up to her to manage the many requests for interviews, discussions etc. that are addressed to Michael Schumacher.

He refuses to give interviews at the track during grand prix weekends and prefers to concentrate entirely on his driving. The only times he expresses himself in public on these occasions are at the official press conferences after qualifying and the race which the first three have to attend under pain of a heavy fine if absent.

He gives interviews during private testing when he has a little free time during the midday break. Journalists who want to interview him have to go to Fiorano, Jerez, Monza etc and often have to wait several months or even a year! She has to look after the schedule for these interviews. *"I chose to do this job for Michael as it gave me a different perspective from journalism,"* she explains. *"It was an opportunity to see things from the other side of the mirror, from the organisation aspect. I miss writing a little but it's a very interesting job."*

Sabine Kemm follows Michael like his shadow at grands prix and private testing. *"Michael is a very easy guy. When he's asked to do this or that he takes a decision and keeps to it. If he doesn't like something he says no and that's that. I appreciate his honesty. He's very demanding and is always trying to improve himself so you have to keep up. I'm never at home and even I have problems trying to get to talk to him for five minutes! The best time is when we're in the car in the morning bringing us to the circuit from the hotel. I go with him every second time and it's a brief moment of calm. Obviously, I often have to say no to proposals he receives and that's what's toughest in this job."*

Willy Weber, Michael Schumacher's manager, came into the Kerpen driver's life in 1988 before hiring him to drive in his F3 team and signing a ten year contract (see also chapter 1).

The most sought-after person in the world

Today aged fifty-seven he looks after everything for his driver - from buying the new car he wants to settling in Switzerland, his marriage etc. He does everything possible to prevent Michael from having the slightest problem so that he can concentrate all his energy on driving. *"I'm the most sought after person in the world,"* is how Willy modestly describes himself!

In the world of Formula 1 all the drivers' managers envy Webber's position, Mr 20%, whose income is estimated at 10 million dollars per year from his driver's contracts and the revenues from the 'Michael Schumacher Collection'. More in fact than most of the F1 drivers without the slightest risk! *"Of course I earn a lot of money,"* confides Willy. *"My contract with Michael ran until December 1999 but has been renewed since then (apparently for five years with a margin reduced from 20 to 10% on business deals). It should be remembered that when Michael signed with me he was nothing. I had a very competitive F3 team that had just won the championship with Joachim Winkelhock. I had to find a new driver and I spotted Michael in Formula König and Formula Ford. I offered him a test drive in one of my cars and he was mighty impressive. I signed him for a few races but soon realised that he was a star of the future. I looked after everything for him and paid him a salary of 2000 Deutschmarks per month. I acted as both team manager and his manager."*

At the time Weber was a well-known Stuttgart businessman. *"I had several hotels and restaurants; I don't know how many but at least thirty-five. I sold most of them in 1995 and kept just a few. I no longer have the time to look after them. I often regret the fact that there are only 24 hours in a day!"*

My office is his office

Things started to get serious for Willy when Michael came into Formula 1. *"In the early days I looked after everything. It killed me! Contacts with the press were especially difficult as there were far too many requests for interviews. So I took on Horst Buchinger at the beginning of 1995. I didn't know him before that but he did a great job. Since the my life has been a whole lot easier."*

Buchinger was let go at the end of 1999 and replaced by Sabine Kehm and the reasons for his departure were never really clarified. It seems that his explanations to the press when he was supposed to speak on behalf of Michael Schumacher, did not truly reflect the driver's wishes during the summer when he was absent from the track convalescing after his Silverstone accident.

"I still continue to look after other details of Michael's life," explains Weber. *"My office is his office. It's impossible to telephone him as he's too busy with Ferrari. I'm like his secretary and I filter his calls. I also take care of his wants. If he wants a new car I look at the prices, the options available, I submit them to him and he decides. He wants to move to Switzerland? I look after the administrative details and find the most beautiful villas. Thus, he wastes a minimum of time and can concentrate on his driving and testing. I supply him with the ideas and options. He decides. He's a very intelligent bloke."*

While his relationship with journalists are among Willy's worst memories his best moments have been those shared with Michael. *"I like souvenirs; those objects that mean something which you guard preciously. He often gives me little things which mean a lot: a helmet after a crash, old racing boots..."*

Over the years the relationship between Willy Weber and Michael Schumacher has become more like a father and son one than that of driver-manager. *"We speak about everything together; we've shared the work. He's a better driven than I am so he drives. I'm a better manager than him so I manage. It's as simple as that."*

Since the beginning Willy Weber has extended his power in F1 as he also manages Ralf Schumacher, Michael's younger brother who made his debut in the Jordan-Peugeot team in 1997 for whom he continued in 1998 after which he joined Williams in 1999. The Weber recipe seems to work as well for the younger as for the elder.

CHAPTER 13

The man behind the driver

While he is literally worshipped in Germany Michael is often denigrated abroad for being an arrogant, cold and calculating driver. He tries to belie this reputation which has certainly improved during his Ferrari years but it is still true that his attitude awakens certain hostilities. The former president of the Italian senate, Ernesto Cossiga, criticised him vehemently just after his world title with Ferrari accusing him of irreverence during the Italian national anthem on the Suzuka rostrum (Michael as is often the case imitated the gestures of an orchestra conductor to direct the choir of Italian mechanics just below him). Cossiga called him 'a pretentious little Bavarian.'

In general, though, while some people remain hostile to the German he seems to be increasingly admired by the public. During his Benetton years he was only really appreciated in Germany but the incredible efforts he has made to help Ferrari get back on top has transformed him into a star in many other countries starting with Italy. Today, the red caps in the colours of the Scuderia or Michael's personal sponsor can be seen on circuits all over the world from Australia to Japan by way of the USA or Great Britain. The Schumacher phenomenon is now a planetary one.

It is impossible to sum up Michael Schumacher in a few lines. To make him out it is indispensable to know his past and to grasp the demands of his work at Ferrari, to which must be added the pressure on his shoulders to prove on the track the work of hundreds of workers and engineers who have spent sleepless nights improving the four-wheeled machine that he drives on Sundays in grands prix. He masks this tension very well but showed a glimpse of it at the 2000 Italian Grand Prix when he burst into tears during the press conference after the race. He had just won this event which put him back into contention in the title chase that many thought was lost (see chapter 8). The emotion generated by seeing thousands of Tifosi massed under the rostrum and the feeling that winning the title was again a real possibility were too strong even for someone as tough as Michael Schumacher.

Self-parodying in the Ferrari camp

He also knows how to enjoy himself. After his 2000 world title he spent most of the Sunday night in the Karaoke bar in the Suzuka Circuit Hotel with Corinna and Mika and Erika Häkkinen. Following his win in Malaysia two weeks later which gave Ferrari its second consecutive Constructors' Championship he put on the long red wig like all the other team members. Not in the austere McLaren ambience would one find such self-parody!

However, between the commercial demands of his sponsors, the time he dedicates to his personal fitness and work on the track with his engineers he does not have a lot of time to lead the quiet family life to which he aspires.

In a few years Michael has become the biggest star in F1 and in the whole of Germany. However, such a quick rise to fame and fortune have wrought very little change in the behaviour of this driver from a modest background.

His values are rock solid and he has kept his feet firmly on the ground in conditions that would have blown the minds of many people. *"I've grown up pretty rapidly since I've been in Formula 1,"* he says. *"My face chan-*

The photographic rights of Corinna and Michael's wedding were given to charity.

ged very quickly during my first years in F1 and often photographers asked me to pose for new portraits as its appearance had altered so much in a few weeks. I've also evolved a lot as a person. On my debuts I hardly dared speak as I was afraid of saying something stupid or revealing team secrets. F1 is so intense that in a year you undergo a series of events that it would take ten years for a normal person to experience. Everything happened to me so quickly at the beginning that I hardly knew who I was any more! I couldn't rest and I didn't understand what was going on. Today I'm more open because I've now understood what F1 is all about. I've got my own viewpoint and I've got much more confidence in myself. "

Ungrateful public opinion

Such is his self-confidence now that it enables him to go through the toughest problems without being affected, hence the reputation for arrogance that has been pinned on him. It hurts. *"I know that not everybody can love me. That's how life is but the worst thing is those journalists who write about me saying I'm arrogant. They take up ten minutes of my time and then go away and try to judge me. I think my problem comes from the fact that I reached the top very quickly. Too quick in any case for people to really get to know me. I think that little by little I'll manage to show who I really am, but it's not easy.*

In Formula 1 you spend most of your time hiding as it's impossible to satisfy everybody. And when you avoid people because you're too busy to speak to them they take it as arrogance. In the paddock my personality is different from the one that my true friends know. I don't think that I'm stand-offish or cold. I don't like arrogant people; I have problems with them and there's no way I could work with such individuals. Above all I try to be honest. It's my life principle and I don't think I've every betrayed it. Honesty gives you better results in life. Either speak the truth or shut up!"

Security and independence

Perhaps part of Michael's reputation for arrogance stems from the huge amount of money he demands to drive for Ferrari. *"For me that money represents security, nothing more. And independence. I think I'm paid for the work I do - but I was happy at the time I earned 450 marks as a trainee mechanic. During my career my salary has gone up bit by bit without that destabilising me. I'm not the kind of guy, as I've read in the press, who wants a Boeing 737 or anything like that. I hate wasting money. For example, I never gamble in casinos. I'm very conservative in my investments and I never play the stock market even though I'd make more money there. In any case once you've got a certain amount then money no longer has the same meaning. I've got*

money and I appreciate it. For me, though, it's time that's freedom, not cash!"

Even if Michael thinks he has got enough dosh in the bank this has not stopped him from negotiating large salary increases during his career. *"It's true,"* he confirms. *"My aim, though, is not to keep this money in the bank. I think that I've got a mission to fulfil thanks to my ability to drive quicker than the others. I feel it's a gift from God and I must use it to help people. This talent is obviously going to bring me a lot of money in the future and I want to use this cash to improve the life of people in misery. I hate poverty especially when children can't eat their fill. I always wanted to do something for them even before I became a star."* This recalls the episode in 1990 when he donated his prize of £20 000 to charity when he was still a young driver with little money (see chapter 1).

Michael is not just a drawing room philanthropist. He works with UNESCO which named him Ambassador for Children in 1996. The German has already financed several projects including a school in Sarajevo which he visited in 1996. It is an activity about which he remains very discreet. *"In the future I hope to be able to use the fact that I'm well-known to draw attention to other humanitarian projects,"* he confides. *"I've got very little time for myself which is why I've decided to trust UNESCO with my donations. I know that part of the money goes into working expenses but I haven't been able to find a better solution. Today when I'm asked to appear on television I say that I want my fees paid directly to it. Because for me, and this may seem arrogant, I don't really care about earning another 10 000 marks. I prefer that people less fortunate than me profit from them."*

Although Michael never reveals anything about his generosity, traces of it can be seen. During the 2002 Hungarian Grand Prix it came out that the German had donated one million euros to people who were victims of the flooding in central Europe.

A generous marriage

In the same spirit Michael and Corinna Schumacher sold the exclusive photographic rights of their wedding for some 600000 Deutschmarks to the magazine Bunte for the benefit of UNESCO. At the time the affair hit the headlines as the rival magazine 'Stern' tried to take a few photos but came up against the white sheets hung round the church while umbrellas effectively prevented any helicopter shots.

In spite of his immense wealth Michael says that he has no real luxury tastes. *"It's true, my tastes are not really very complicated. You know I'm a normal guy trying to live a normal life. I like being at home with Corinna and sha-*

ring a meal that she's cooked. We haven't got staff in the house and we do our own shopping. My favourite books are action novels and I like listening to Phil Collins or Michael Jackson although I'm now beginning to develop a passion for opera."

Plane haven!

The Ferrari driver has given himself a few presents like a Bugatti and a new private jet. For several years he used a little eight-seater Cessna Citation and in 1997 he bought a superb Challenger 601P worth around 100 million francs and adapted to his tastes with a bedroom and bathroom. The plane is big enough to stand up in and has an autonomy of 9000 kilometres. *"Obviously, it's a fairly costly piece of luxury,"* he admits. *"All the more so as two pilots have to paid full time but it's vital for my work, though. At the French Grand Prix I was doing private testing in Italy until 15h00 on Thursday afternoon and three hours later I was supposed to be at Magny-Cours for Ferrari promotional activity. So you understand I couldn't live this type of life without my plane. Frequent travelling involves so much discomfort and is so tiring. I'm sure that numerous drivers wouldn't have stayed so long in F1 were it not for their private planes."*

Contemplating the stars

Michael Schumacher insist on the simplicity of his life and his love of nature. *"When you begin motor sport you think that a good car will fulfil all your desires,"* he explains. *"When you have it you realise in fact that it doesn't fulfil anything. It's nice to drive, that's all. Today, my secret dreams have nothing to do with motor racing or with a third or fourth world title. It's what I see around me that really gives me a buzz. I love sitting on the balcony in the evening watching the reflection of the moon in the sea. Sometimes Corinna and I go down to the beach and play with the kids. When the weather is bad we're not disturbed by anybody. That's when I'm happy. I like sitting at night contemplating the stars. Space fascinates me. I've got deep religious beliefs and I think that nature represents all that is most remarkable on this earth."*

Do his beliefs help him to face up to the fear of an accident, an unavoidable question when talking to a driver. *"This job pleases me and I get great fun out of it,"* he explained to the British journalist Derek Allsop in his book 'Formula for Success.' *"It's dangerous, that's obvious. All top level sporting activities are risky and so is getting into your car and going for a drive. In my opinion motor racing is not dangerous provided you keep within certain reasonable limits. After the deaths of Roland Ratzenberger and Ayrton Senna I thought seriously about my future in*

F1. I didn't know if I could drive normally in the next race and it was only after private testing at Silverstone that I realised things were all right. First of all I felt a bit scared but then I upped the pace bit by bit. I think that in getting older you become more concerned with these problems. I've never had a serious accident in my career. The first time I injured myself was in F1 in the 1991 Japanese Grand Prix. As soon as I went back to the pit and got into the spare I was half-a-second quicker! As long as I understand why I go off then I've got no problems."

At Imola in 1995 he had a big accident in the race. *"I'm never afraid in the car. That day I said to myself: 'watch out, this is going to hurt.' Nothing more and then bang, I hit! It stopped there. There's never been a moment when I've said I'll stop; this sport is too dangerous for me."*

Naturally Michael lived through this moment's hesitation after his accident in the 1999 British Grand Prix which kept him away from the track for seven races. Initially it was described as not being too serious and the German wanted to get back behind the wheel after less than a month. The doctors advised against it and finally he had to wait another two weeks to find out that his leg was still very painful. *"After such an impact you ask yourself what's the use of going on taking such risks. In the hospital I felt like stopping,"* he admits. *"An accident like that makes you aware of the danger of the job which you often forget or deliberately ignore. Naturally, you call yourself into question. But that way of seeing things doesn't last very long. The desire to get behind the steering wheel was far too strong."*

Relative happiness

There is no doubt that the German is a serious individual. He smiles rarely and bursts out laughing even less. Does he really enjoy life? Is he happy? *"Relatively happy, yes,"* he answers. *"I like my job. I like driving. This being said I don't know how long I'm going to continue. For me beating the record for the number of world titles was not an aim in itself. I don't pay a lot of heed to records. When I'm retired it'll perhaps be nice to have a look and see what ones I've beaten; but they're not an aim in themselves for me. I'll continue driving as long as it gives me pleasure. If between now and then I've got five, six or seven titles...great, but I don't let it bother me. When I say I'm relatively happy it's because my life isn't always pleasant due to my popularity. Overall, things are pretty good and I'm not complaining. OK sometimes I get fed up with all the attention that's concentrated on me. I'd prefer to take my car and drive home quietly. Since I've moved to Switzerland things are a lot better. It's wrong to say that I never have fun.*

167

Sometimes I let my hair down in a discotheque like any other young person."

Discretion allied to success

At the start of his career in 1992 he was often seen at the bars and discos around the circuits. On the evening following the Portguese Grand Prix he stayed at 'Coconuts', the famous Cascais night club until 5 a.m letting it all hang out on the dance floor with a group of friends he'd met that evening. His growing popularity has driven him to be more discreet. *"When I was doing karting and F3 a bunch of us used to go out after practice. Of course, I miss that. My life's different nowadays and I'm happy to go out when I'm far away from the track, at home. For example, every New Year I meet up with the same group of friends. In 1996, one of them tried to push me into the outside swimming pool. He managed finally but I made sure he came in with me! The water was exactly 2 degrees. Freezing. I got a bad cold after that incident! This is the side of my personality that nobody knows. When I work, I work. Full stop. I try and keep my private life apart, far from the public eye."*

He admits that he does not party very often and drinks very little alcohol. He follows a strict diet looked after by his Hindu trainer/physiotherapist Balbir Singh. *"Of course, I like having a little drink from time to time especially with friends at the end of the year. In general from 1st January I don't drink alcohol. As my birthday falls on 3rd January all my friends always ask me to have a beer and I have to say no."*

Hell in Monaco

It was this need for privacy that finally drove the German out of Monaco. Even if the Principality is a tax haven it became hell for someone as popular as popular as him! *"Monte Carlo became unliveable for me,"* he says. *"Each time I went jogging or out in a boat with friends people recognised me and came running. When we arrived in the harbour they massed to see us mooring or leaving if they were not following us in another boat. I don't like to feel the crowd pressing around me. And so I act to keep them away and yet again I'm said to be arrogant. I remember that once Corinna was in the supermarket and I was waiting in my car. I was on the phone when someone recognised me. People gathered around the car and began to bang on the closed windows. It was unbearable. A single person would never have dared do that but when people are in groups then life becomes hell for me. I had to find somewhere calmer to live, hence Switzerland. There I'm left in peace when I go for a walk. When I jog there are no cameras around and that's the kind of life I want to lead."*

Betrayed by his wig!

For Michael life in Monaco became so unbearable that the couple had to hide during the day and only go out at night. He even tried camouflage! *"One day I was going to Germany to see my brother race. I put on a wig with long hair and black glasses. On the road when I stopped to fill up the cashier in the filling station gave me change saying 'have a good weekend Mr. Schumacher.' When I arrived at the circuit people all around me said: 'Look it's Michael Schumacher.' I was so ashamed that I didn't know where to put myself!"*

And so Michael, Corinna, their two children, their terrier Jenny, their dog Puce and their two Belgian shepherds set up in a rented 15 room villa with a swimming pool. Because of Swiss laws on immigration they were not authorised to buy the house. Michael was not too disappointed as it was not exactly the villa of his dreams. *"In fact, I was looking for a farm to breed horses. I love animals. I also wanted to be beside a lake with a view on the mountains. It wasn't easy. I visited over fifty properties before choosing the one at Vufflens-le-Château. It was not exactly what I wanted but the only way was to live there for a few years and look around in peace. In any case I'm not often at home. Last year I think my trips added up to 300 days!"*

In 2002, Michael and his wife decided to buy a huge property in the Appenzel canton in the German-speaking part of Switzerland. It had a lot of land for horse riding and a superb farm that had to be renovated. *"It's near Zurich airport and people speak German. It's better for our children; it's our culture,"* explained the German. A project was developed including the creation of a heliport and various sporting installations but finally it was abandoned because of opposition from the local ecologists.

Chased by farmers

After more than a year in Switzerland Michael had enough time to see the advantages and disadvantages of his new home. *"At first I found it really great. I could go for a walk on Saturdays, go to the vegetable market in Morges, the little village near me. Nobody bothered me and there were few requests for autographs. But lately things are not as rosy. I don't know why. Certainly because I'm leading the 1997 world championship and everybody in Switzerland knows I live in the region. People are no longer surprised to see me and approach me more easily. Sometimes it gets a bit boring. In July I went for a ride with Alain Prost who lives five kilometres away. After a couple of minutes two peasants stopped their work and chased us in their car to get two autographs. Such situations may seem comical from the outside but when you have to put up with them all the time, it's anything but."*

Michael Schumacher had to have some work done around his villa which some people described as a wall. *"It's not a wall, much more like a fence. It's because of my dogs. My German shepherds are pretty big and I don't want them to hurt anybody. The fence is for my neighbours' safety, not mine (laughs). On the other hand it's true that I've done some work on the house. It's not mine as I have to stay in Switzerland for five years before I can buy something."*

Taxwise the Swiss have been understanding. In Vufflens it is said that the German pays practically no tax. *"I want to do everything perfectly legally. OK, it's true that I pay more tax than in Monaco where I didn't pay any. I've come to an arrangement with the Vufflens commune. I pay tax on the salaries I receive in Switzerland, that's all. You must remember that I still pay a lot of tax in Germany where there is a law that obliges German nationals to pay their taxes in the country until ten years after their departure. They tax me on one eighth of my salary arguing that I drive in two grands prix out of sixteen in Germany and that I'm paid for sixteen grands prix. They forget all about the rest of the work like testing etc. But that's how it is. I don't want to stir up trouble, I want things to be in order."*

Whatever his problems with the German tax authorities Michael loves his country. The colours on his helmet include the three in the German flag. *"To design my helmet I took the German colours and added a little blue. I wanted to have the national colours and I asked a friend to create a design with them. He brought me the blue top with the stars that I've kept. On the sides, though, I changed the motif as I didn't like it very much. That was in 1986 and since then I haven't changed anything."* Since then nothing changed... until 2000 when he modified the top changing from blue to red - his helmet was too similar to that of his team-mate Rubens Barrichello. Seen from the on-board cameras on the rollbar it was impossible to distinguish the two drivers. Suddenly Michael Schumacher changed to red at the Monaco Grand Prix: a colour that seems to have brought him luck!

With his move to the Swiss German region cancelled Michael has to stay at Vufflens-le-Château a bit longer where he is well-integrated and his children go the school in Rolle not far away.

He also participates in the life of local associations. Thus, he offered a playground to the Vufflens-le-Château commune and he often plays football with the Echichens team from a little village nearby. He likes the team for which he organises an annual day out. In 2001, the German organised an in-door karting day in Payerne abou fifty kilometres away. He did everything himself and paid all the expenses for the members of his football club and their families. In 2002, he invited them all to the Spanish Grand Prix. He arranged with the organisers to have enough passes and all the team was able to visit the pits in the evening after practice. It was another example of his personal generosity.

The German takes very little advantage of the mountains that surround his home. He is too well-known in Europe and prefers to go to Norway in December or January to ski on the slopes in peace. He has bought a beautiful chalet in the region.

Today Michael and Corinna are the parents of Gina Maria and Mick Junior. The German has always said that he wanted a family more than anything else in the world and the two births have filled him with happiness.

Today Michael and Corinna and the parents of little Gina Maria. He said that he wanted a family above all else in the world and her birth filled him with joy. *"I was there with Corinna when she was born. It was something much stronger than winning the world championship; you can believe me. My real ambition is to have a family and raise my children. What more could you ask for than to have children in good health and to bring them up well. Doing this is much more important than winning any world championship,"* he summed up. Yet again the man takes precedence over the driver.

Michael Schumacher's complete honour list as of September 1st 2002

1973 - 1987 Karting

1984   German Junior Champion

1985   German Junior Champion
Takes part in Junior World Championship

1986   3rd in German Championship
3rd in European Championship

1987   German Champion
European Champion

1988   Wins Formula König Championship
6th in Formule Ford 1600 German Championship
2nd in Formule Ford 1600 European Championship

1989   Takes part in the Formula 3 German Championship on Reynard from WTS Motorsport

Date	Track	Qualification	Race
March 18th	Hockenheim (non-champ.)	4	2
April 1st	Hockenheim (non-champ.)	4	1
April 16th	Hockenheim	2	3
April 30th	Nürburgring	5	3
May 28th	Avus	5	3
June 11th	Brno	8	5
June 18th	Zeltweg	1	1
July 2nd	Hockenheim	2	3
July 9th	Wunstorf	6	12
July 29th	Hockenheim	4	19
August 6th	Diepholz	4	4
September 3rd	Nürburgring	6	5
September 23rd	Nürburgring	1	1
September 30th	Hockenheim	2	3
November 26th	Macao (non-champ.)	6	retired

Championship final Classification: second ex-aequo (163 points)

1990 Takes part in the Formula 3 German Championship with WTS Motorsport

Date	Track	Qualification	Race
March 24th	Hockenheim (non-champ.)	2	1
March 31st	Zolder	1	retired
April 7th	Hockenheim	1	19
April 21st	Nürburgring	22	5
May 5th	Avus	2	1
June 3rd	Wunstorf	1	1
June 30th	Norisring	4	2
July 14th	Zeltweg	1	1
August 4th	Diepholz	7	1
August 18th	Nürburgring	1	1
September 1st	Nürburgring	1	4
October 13th	Hockenheim	2	2
November 25th	Macao (non-champ.)	2	1
December 2nd	Fuji (non-champ.)	2	1

Championship final Classification: 1st (148 points)

1990 Takes part in the Sport Prototype World Championship with Sauber-Mercedes

Date	Track	Qualification	Race
May 20th	Silverstone	disqualified	
July 22nd	Dijon	3	2
August 19th	Nürburgring	2	2
October 22nd	Mexico-City	2	1

Championship final Classification: 5th (21 points)

1991 Takes part in the Sport Prototype World Championship with Sauber-Mercedes

Date	Track	Qualification	Race
April 14th	Suzuka	3	retired
May 5th	Monza	6	retired
May 19th	Silverstone	5	2
June 22/23rd	Le Mans	4	5
August 18th	Nürburgring	5	retired
September 15th	Magny-Cours	3	retired
October 6th	Mexico-City	2	retired
October 27th	Autopolis	6	1

Championship final Classification: 9th (43 points).

1991 Takes part in the Japanese Formula 3000 Championship with Team Le Mans Ralt

Date	Track	Qualification	Race
July 28th	Sugo	2	2

1991 Takes part in the Formula 1 World Championship with Team Jordan-Ford

Date	Track	Qualification	Race
August 24th	Spa	7	retired

1991   Takes part in the Formula 1World Championship with the Benetton-Ford team

Date	Track	Qualification	Race
September 8th	Monza	7	5
September 22nd	Estoril	10	6
September 29th	Barcelone	5	6
October 20th	Suzuka	9	retired
November 3rd	Adelaïde	6	retired

Drivers Championship final Classification: 12th (4 points)

1992   Takes part in the Formula 1 World Championship with the Benetton-Ford team

Date	Track	Qualification	Race
March 1st	Kyalami	6	4
Maerch 22nd	Mexico City	3	3
April 5th	Interlagos	5	3
May 3rd	Barcelona	2	2
May 17th	Imola	5	retired
May 31st	Monaco	6	4
June 14th	Montréal	5	2
July 5th	Magny-Cours	5	retired
July 12th	Silverstone	4	4
July 26th	Hockenheim	6	3
August 16th	Hungaroring	4	retired
August 30th	Spa	3	1
September 13th	Monza	6	3
September 27th	Estoril	5	7
October 25th	Suzuka	5	retired
November 8th	Adelaïde	5	2

Drivers Championship final Classification: 3rd (53 points)

1993   Takes part in the Formula 1 World Championship with the Benetton-Ford team

Date	Track	Qualification	Race
March 14th	Kyalami	3	retired
March 28th	Interlagos	4	3
April 11th	Donington	3	retired
April 25th	Imola	3	2
May 9th	Barcelone	4	3
May 23rd	Monaco	2	retired
June 13th	Montréal	3	2
July 4th	Magny-Cours	7	3
July 11th	Silverstone	3	2
July 25th	Hockenheim	3	2
August 15th	Hungaroring	3	retired
August 29th	Spa	3	2
September 12th	Monza	5	retired
September 26th	Estoril	6	1
October 24th	Suzuka	4	retired
November 7th	Adélaïde	4	retired

Drivers Championship final Classification: 4th (52 points)

1994 Takes part in the Formula 1 World Championship with the Benetton-Ford team
WORLD CHAMPION

Date	Track	Qualification	Race
March 27th	Interlagos	2	1
April 1st	Aïda	2	1
May 1st	Imola	2	1
May 15th	Monaco	1	1
May 29th	Barcelone	1	2
June 12th	Montréal	1	1
July 3rd	Magny-Cours	3	1
July 10th	Silverstone	2	disqualified
July 31st	Hockenheim	4	retired
August 14th	Hungaroring	1	1
August 28th	Spa	2	disqualified
October 16th	Jerez	1	1
November 6th	Suzuka	1	2
November 13th	Adélaïde	2	retired

(*Note*: Michael Schumacher was not authorized to start in Monza and Estoril)

Drivers Championship final Classification: 1st (92 points)

1995 Takes part in the Formula 1 World Championship with the Benetton-Renault team
WORLD CHAMPION

Date	Track	Qualification	Race
March 26th	Interlagos	2	1
April 9th	Buenos Aires	3	3
April 30th	Imola	1	retired
May 14th	Barcelone	1	1
May 28th	Monaco	2	1
June 11th	Montréal	1	5
July 2nd	Magny-Cours	2	1
July 16th	Silverstone	2	retired
July 30th	Hockenheim	2	1
August 13th	Hungaroring	3	11
August 27th	Spa	16	1
September 10th	Monza	2	retired
September 24th	Estoril	3	2
October 1st	Nürburgring	3	1
October 22nd	Aïda	3	1
October 29th	Suzuka	1	1
November 12th	Adélaïde	3	retired

Drivers Championship final Classification: 1st (102 points)

1996 Takes part in the Formula 1 World Championship with the Ferrari team

Date	Track	Qualification	Race
March 10th	Melbourne	4	retired
March 31st	Interlagos	4	3
April 7th	Buenos Aires	2	retired
April 28th	Nürburgring	3	2

May 5th	Imola	1	2
May 19th	Monaco	1	retired
June 2nd	Barcelone	3	1
June 16th	Montréal	3	retired
June 30th	Magny-Cours	1	retired
July 14th	Silverstone	3	retired
July 28th	Hockenheim	3	4
August 11th	Hungaroring	1	9
August25th	Spa	3	1
September 8th	Monza	3	1
Setember 22nd	Estoril	4	3
October 13th	Suzuka	3	2

Drivers Championship final Classification: 3rd (59 points)

1997 Takes part in the Formula 1 World Championship with the Ferrari team

Date	Track	Qualification	Race
March 9th	Melbourne	3	2
March 30th	Interlagos	2	5
April 13th	Buenos Aires	4	retired
April 27th	Imola	3	2
May 11th	Monaco	2	1
May 25th	Barcelone	7	4
June 15th	Montréal	1	1
June 29th	Magny-Cours	1	1
July 13th	Silverstone	4	retired
July 27th	Hockenheim	3	2
August10th	Hungaroring	1	4
August 24th	Spa	3	1
September 7th	Monza	9	6
September 21st	A1-Ring	9	6
September 28th	Nürburgring	5	retired
October 12th	Suzuka	2	1
Octobre 26th	Jerez	2	retired

Drivers Championship final Classification: -
(*Note*: Michael Schumacher (78 points) was excluded from the final classification of the Drivers Championship following a faulty manoeuvre on Jacques Villeneuve during the European Grand Prix in Jerez).

1998 Takes part in the Formula 1 World Championship with the Ferrari team

Date	Track	Qualification	Race
March 8th	Melbourne	3	retried
March 29th	Interlagos	4	3
April 12th	Buenos Aires	2	1
April 26th	Imola	3	2
May 10th	Barcelone	3	3
May 24th	Monaco	4	10
June 7th	Montréal	3	1
June 28th	Magny-Cours	2	1
July 12th	Silverstone	2	1
July 26th	A1-Ring	4	3
August 2nd	Hockenheim	9	5

August 16th	Hungaroring	3	1
August 30th	Spa	4	retrired
September 13th	Monza	1	1
September 27th	Nürburgring	1	2
November 1st	Suzuka	1	retrired

Drivers Championship final Classification: 2nd (86 points)

1999 Takes part in the Formula 1 World Championship with the Ferrari team

Date	Track	Qualification	Race
March 7th	Melbourne	3	8
April 11th	Interlagos	4	2
May 2nd	Imola	3	1
May 16th	Monaco	2	1
May 30th	Barcelone	2	3
June 13th	Montréal	1	retired
June 27th	Magny-Cours	6	5
July 11th	Silverstone	2	retired
July 25th	A1-Ring	-	forfeit
August 1st	Hockenheim	-	forfeit
August 15th	Hungaroring	-	forfeit
August 29th	Spa	-	forfeit
September 12th	Monza	-	forfeit
September 26th	Nürburgring	-	forfeit
October 17th	Sepang	1	2
October 31th	Suzuka	1	2

Drivers Championship final Classification: 5th (44 points)

2000 Takes part in the Formula 1 World Championship with the Ferrari team
WORLD CHAMPION

Date	Track	Qualification	Race
March 12th	Melbourne	3	1
March 26th	Interlagos	3	1
April 9th	Imola	2	1
April 23rd	Silverstone	5	3
May 7th	Barcelone	1	5
May 21st	Nürburgring	2	1
June 4th	Monaco	1	retired
June 18th	Montréal	1	1
July 2nd	Magny-Cours	1	retired
July 16th	A1-Ring	4	retired
July 30th	Hockenheim	2	retired
August 13th	Hungaroring	1	2
August 27th	Spa	4	2
September 7th	Monza	1	1
September 24th	Indianapolis	1	1
October 8th	Suzuka	1	1
October 22nd	Sepang	1	1

Drivers Championship final Classification: 1st (108 points)

2001 Takes part in the Formula 1 World Championship with the Ferrari team
WORLD CHAMPION

Date	Track	Qualification	Race
March 4th	Melbourne	1	1
March 18th	Sepang	1	1
April 1st	Interlagos	1	2
April 15th	Imola	4	retired
April 29th	Barcelone	1	1
May 13th	A1-Ring	1	2
May 27th	Monaco	2	1
June 10th	Montréal	1	2
June 24th	Nürburgring	1	1
July 1st	Magny-Cours	2	1
July 15th	Silverstone	1	2
July 29th	Hockenheim	4	retired
August 19th	Hungaroring	1	1
September 2nd	Spa	3	1
September 16th	Monza	3	4
September 30th	Indianapolis	1	2
October 14th	Suzuka	1	1

Drivers Championship final Classification: 1st (123 points)

2002 Takes part in the Formula 1 World Championship with the Ferrari team
WORLD CHAMPION

Date	Circuit	Qualifications	Course
March 3rd	Melbourne	2	1
March 17th	Sepang	1	3
March 31st	Interlagos	2	1
April 14th	Imola	1	1
April 28th	Barcelone	1	1
May 12th	A1-Ring	3	1
May 26th	Monaco	3	2
June 9th	Montréal	2	1
June 23rd	Nürburgring	3	2
July 7th	Silverstone	3	1
July 21st	Magny-Cours	2	1
July 28th	Hockenheim	1	1
August 18th	Hungaroring	2	2
September 1st	Spa	1	1

Drivers Championship Classification after fourteen races out of seventeen: 1st (122 points). Cannot be surpassed and has clinched the World Title in Magny-Cours.